CW00741689

YORKSHIRE DAYS

by

Nicholas Rhea

HUTTON PRESS
1995

Published by
The Hutton Press Ltd.,
130 Canada Drive, Cherry Burton,
Beverley, East Yorkshire, HU17 7SB

Printed and bound by
Clifford Ward & Co. (Bridlington) Ltd.,
55 West Street, Bridlington, East Yorkshire, YO15 3DZ

ISBN 1 872167 70 5

CONTENTS

Page

BOOKS BY *Peter N. Walker/Nicholas Rhea*

CRIME FICTION
The 'Carnaby' Series (1967-84)
Carnaby and the hijackers
Carnaby and the gaolbreakers
Carnaby and the assassins
Carnaby and the conspirators
Carnaby and the saboteurs
Carnaby and the eliminators
Carnaby and the demonstrators
Carnaby and the infiltrators
Carnaby and the kidnappers
Carnaby and the counterfeiters
Carnaby and the campaigners
Fatal accident (1970)
Panda One on duty (1971)
Special duty (1971)
Identification Parade (1972)
Panda One investigates (1973)
Major incident (1974)
The Dovingsby death (1975)
Missing from home (1977)
The MacIntyre plot (1977)
Witchcraft for Panda One (1978)
Target criminal (1978)
The Carlton plot (1980)
Siege for Panda One (1981)
Teenage cop (1982)
Robber in a mole trap (1985)
False alibi (1991)
Grave secrets (1992)
Family Ties (1994) *Nicholas Rhea*
Written as Christopher Coram
A call to danger (1968)
A call to die (1969)
Death in Ptarmigan Forest (1970)
Death on the motorway (1973)
Murder by the lake (1975)
Murder beneath the trees (1979)
Prisoner on the dam (1982)
Prisoner on the run (1985)
Written as Tom Ferris
Espionage for a lady (1969)
Written as Andrew Arncliffe
Murder after the holidays (1985)
NON-FICTION
The courts of law (1971)
Punishment (1972)

Murders and Mysteries from the North York
    Moors (1988)
Murders and mysteries from the Yorkshire
    Dales (1991)
Folk tales from the North York Moors (1990)
Folk stories from the Yorkshire Dales (1991)
Portrait of the North York Moors (1985)
    as Nicholas Rhea
Heartbeat of Yorkshire (1993)
    as Nicholas Rhea
Folk tales from York and the Wolds (1992)
Folk stories from the Lake District (1993)
The Story of the Police Mutual
    Assurance Society (1993)
The 'Constable' series
    Written as Nicholas Rhea
Constable on the hill (1979)
Constable on the prowl (1980)
Constable around the village (1981)
Constable across the moors (1982)
Constable in the dale (1983)
Constable by the sea (1985)
Constable along the lane (1986)
Constable through the meadow (1988)
Constable at the double (1988)
Constable in disguise (1989)
Constable through the heather (1990)
Constable beside the stream (1991)
Constable around the green (1993)
Constable beneath the trees
Heartbeat Omnibus I (1992)
Heartbeat Omnibus II (1993)
Heartbeat — Constable among the heather
    (1992)
Heartbeat — Constable across the moor
    (1993)
Heartbeat — Constable on call (1993)
Heartbeat — Constable around the Green
    (1994)
'Emmerdale' titles
Written as James Ferguson
A friend in need (1987)
Divided loyalties (1988)
Wives and lovers (1989)
Book of country lore (1988)
Official companion (1988)
Emmerdale's Yorkshire (1990)

4

INTRODUCTION

The people of Yorkshire love their special days. Whether it is a birthday, an egg jawping day, Ebor Day or a saint's day, the folk of England's largest county make an occasion of it.

This is a collection of days which either have been, or still are, celebrated within Yorkshire's boundaries. Many are honoured outside Yorkshire while some may be known only within the county; several may have fallen into disuse while some are very new, such as Yorkshire Day, instituted in 1975. Others like Nickanan Night, Chaff-Riddling Eve or Backward Bean Day may not be widely known but all within these pages have some association with Yorkshire. The list may not be complete; I hope to discover other Yorkshire days.

Most are included by calendar month, with moveable feasts mentioned in the month usually associated with them. Some of our more curious days feature at the end of the book, while our weekday customs are shown at the beginning.

The influence of the Catholic church is very prominent, this being lessened by the institution of the Church of England following the Reformation; it will also be seen that some days are prefixed with 'Old', such as Old Christmas Day, Old Twelfth Day and Old Midsummer Day. This arises through changes to the calendar; Julius Caesar's Julian calendar was inaccurate and over the centuries the seasons became mis-placed, the time of the spring equinox being a guide. It occurred on 25 March at the time of Caesar, but had slipped to 11 March by the time of Pope Gregory XIII (1502-1585).

In 1582, Pope Gregory made the necessary corrections by removing ten days to re-instate the seasons' timetable — 5 October become 15 October and thus ten days were suppressed, with 29 February making further adjustments every four years. His calendar is the Gregorian Calendar.

England, however, being newly Protestant, suspected some kind of Catholic plot and refused to accept the changes. European countries used Gregory's calendar but it took England, along with

5

Scotland, almost two hundred years to accept it. Eventually, his calendar was accepted in 1752 by which time eleven days had to be cancelled — 3 September became 13 September that year, and there were riots because some people thought they had been cheated of eleven days of their lives.

The beginning of the legal year was changed from 25 March to 1 January — but a lot of Englishfolk steadfastly refused to accept the changes. They ignored the missing days and continued to celebrate important occasions on the days they would have been celebrated had the calendar **not** been changed.

Miscalculations occurred, and in some cases, those eleven days have become ten, twelve, or some other figure. Even now, some Yorkshire people celebrate Martinmas on 23 November instead of 11 November and our calendar includes days like Old Christmas Day, Old Midsummer Day and the unfortunately titled Old Lady Day. In these pages, therefore, the term 'old' refers to the Julian calendar, mindful of the necessary adjustment of around ten or eleven days, while the 'new' calendar is the Gregorian, the one currently in use.

Nicholas Rhea
June 1995

YORKSHIRE DAYS

Days of the Week

Our birthday is the most important event in our life. The day we enter this world is of enormous significance and there are verses to remind us of the merits of particular birthdays.

> "Monday's child is fair of face,
> Tuesday's child is full of grace;
> Wednesday's child is full of woe,
> Thursday's child has far to go;
> Friday's child is loving and giving,
> Saturday's child works hard for a living,
> But the child that is born on the Sabbath Day
> Is bonny and blithe and good and gay."

The word 'gay' here means happy, charming or carefree, unlike the modern interpretation of the word which implies homosexuality.

> "A Monday's bairn'll grow up fair,
> A Tuesday's yan i'grace through prayer,
> A Wednesday's bairn has monny a pain,
> A Thosday's bairn weean't bahde at heeam,
> A Friday's bairn is good and sweet,
> A Setterday's warks fro morn til neet,
> But a Sunday's bairn through life is blest
> An' seear i' t'end wi' t'saints will rest."

There were other important days in a child's life. One was when to cut babies' finger nails or toe nails. This was not done until the child was twelve months old, otherwise he or she would become a thief. If the nails grew too long, the mother had to bite them rather than cut them. Yorkshire folk believed that the cutting of children's nails had to be done on certain days if good fortune was to be maintained:

> "Better t'bairn had ne'er been born,
> Than cut its nails on a Sunday morn.
> Cut 'em o' Monday, cut 'em for health;

Cut 'em o' Tuesday, cut 'em for wealth;
Cut 'em o' Wednesday, cut 'em for news;
Cut 'em o' Thosday, thoo cuts for new shoes;
Cut 'em o' Friday, thoo cuts 'em for sorrow;
Cut 'em o' Saturday, t'bairn'll nivver need borrow;
Cut 'em o' Sunday, it had better be deead,
For ill-luck an' evil'll lig on its heead."

Sneezing during the week also has its verses and one which applies to most of England goes: "Monday for danger, Tuesday kiss a stranger, Wednesday for a letter, Thursday for something better, Friday for sorrow, Saturday — see your lover tomorrow. But sneeze on a Sunday morning fasting, enjoy your true love for everlasting." It was also thought healthy to sneeze after a meal.

Similarly, there are good and bad days for marriage — unlucky days include St. Thomas' Day, (21 December), Childermas (28 December), Maundy Thursday and St. Swithins (15 July). Monday and Tuesday are good days for a wedding, with Wednesday being the finest as this verse shows:

"Monday for wealth,
Tuesday for health,
Wednesday the best day of all,
Thursday for losses,
Friday for crosses,
And Saturday no luck at all."

Oddly enough, Saturday is now the day when most marriages occur.

***

Even now, Yorkshire folk enjoy a routine based on the days of the week. This was especially so for women — Monday was washing day, Tuesday was ironing day, Wednesday was baking day, Thursday was for dusting and tidying upstairs, while Friday was for dusting and tidying downstairs, as well as being pay day and bath night. Saturday was another baking day and Sunday was a day of rest and reflection. No work was done because best clothes were worn and attendance at church or chapel was of great importance.

A Yorkshirewoman who did not complete her washing on a Monday was thought slovenly and there is a verse which says:

"Them that wash on Monday,
Have a whole week to dry;

8

Them that wash on Tuesday
Are not so much awry;
Them that wash on Wednesday
May get their clothes clean;
Them that wash on Thursday
Are not so much too mean;
Them that wash on Friday
Wash for their need;
Them that wash on Saturday
Are clarty-paps indeed!"

Those who washed on Sundays were considered too dreadful even to be mentioned in this verse.

Day by Day

Sunday

In Yorkshire, several superstitions applied to Sundays. Children born on Sundays were believed gifted and lucky, sometimes with the power to divine the future. Throughout the North of England, it was thought a child born on Sunday would have a good, happy and successful life and that he or she would never become a victim of enemies. Calves born in Yorkshire during Sunday were also reckoned to be lucky!

A woman, after giving birth, was advised to rise from the birthing bed on Sunday to resume her normal life — Sunday was the best day for a return to normality by both mother and child. If a person was ill, it was thought that cures started on Sunday would be successful. However, it was unlucky to put clean sheets on a bed on a Sunday and if a bed is turned on a Sunday, it will cause the user to have bad dreams. It's also unlucky to cut your toe nails, finger nails or hair on a Sunday — "Best nivver to be born than to be Sunday shorn."

One should never plan the future on a Sunday and anyone singing a wrong note in a church service could expect to have their Sunday dinner burnt!

Another Yorkshire belief was that funerals should not occur on Sundays, probably because they attracted the attention of the devil, and if a grave is left open on a Sunday, it is said to yawn for another corpse; it means a second death in the parish will soon follow.

However, Sunday was a good day for setting eggs under a clocker

9

(a broody hen) if you wanted the best brood, but Sunday is not a good day for picking hazel nuts. A new moon on a Sunday means bad weather as well as bad luck. In North Yorkshire, to sneeze after Sunday dinner meant you would enjoy your true love for ever.

Monday

In Yorkshire mining areas, Monday was Collier Monday because some miners took the day off after a hectic weekend.

Monday is a bad day to meet anyone with flat feet especially when starting a journey, beds should not be turned and pigs should not be killed because this causes the meat to shrink in the pot! It is a good day for cutting hair, however, and also for getting married.

Tuesday

Children born on Tuesday are blessed with good looks although the Scots believe they would be solemn and sad. A child's nails and hair may be cut on a Tuesday, but in some parts of the north, it was bad luck to meet a left-handed man on any day except Tuesday. To sneeze on Tuesday means you will soon kiss a stranger and it's a splendid day upon which to marry, bringing health to the bride and groom.

Wednesday

Wednesday was called Wolting day in some parts of Yorkshire. Wolt means 'to tilt' and the reason might be that Wednesday tilted the week into its second half? Children born on Wednesday are thought to lead sad lives, except in Scotland where they are merry and glad. It's not the best of days to cut children's hair or nails, but not particularly unlucky either. To sneeze on Wednesday means you'll get a letter and it's the luckiest day of the week for marriage.

Thursday

Every Thursday at 11 am, the Bellman of Ripon sounds his bell in the market place to formally open trading. Children born on Thursday are likely to be very successful, except in Scotland where they may become thieves.

It is not a bad day to cut children's hair or nails, while to sneeze on Thursday heralds good fortune. Thursday weddings result in sad losses, with Maundy Thursday being a very gloomy day for marriage.

Friday

Friday is called Fettling Day because the house was dusted, cleaned and made tidy after the week's activities. Generally, it is the unluckiest day of the week, with Friday 13 being most unlucky, and Friday 13 May being too terrible to contemplate. Oddly enough, it is not a bad day upon which to be born, unless you are a lamb! Children born on Fridays are loving and giving, but no child should be weaned on a Friday; Friday lambs seldom do well!

In some seaside villages, to turn a bed on a Friday meant a ship would overturn at sea, while inland, parents would not call a doctor to a sick child on a Friday, unless it was a real emergency.

The cutting of hair and nails was fraught with bad fortune, and marrying on Friday was sure to result in sadness, with Good Friday being the worst possible day to wed. So far as weddings are concerned, an old verse says:

"Deearn't o' Friday buy yer ring,
O' Friday, deearn't put t' spurrings in,
Deearnn't wed o' Friday — think o' this,
Nowther blue nor green mun match yer driss."

Spurrings is an old word for publication of the banns of marriage, while a driss means dress.

This is also a bad day for moving house. Even now, Yorkshire folk say, "Friday flit, short sit" meaning that those who move house on Friday will soon be looking for new accommodation.

In rural Yorkshire, love-sick youths and girls would go out silently on Friday at midnight to pick nine female holly leaves; these were tied with nine knots in a three cornered handkerchief and placed under the pillow upon going to bed. It was then thought the future spouse would appear in a dream. This is also a Dumb Cake Eating Day —see 20 January.

Washing clothes on a Friday was regarded as slovenly and only to be done in extreme cases; this old verse being often quoted:

"Wash on Friday, wash in need,
Wash on Saturday, a slut indeed!"

11

To sneeze on a Friday means impending sorrow but in the North Riding of Yorkshire there used to be a curious Friday custom, but only for virgins. After becoming engaged, a girl would ensure fruitful childbearing by going into the harvest field at night to draw straws from the stooks. For every son she desired, she drew wheaten straw; for daughters, she drew oats. These were plaited into a garter and worn around her leg from that Friday until the following Monday morning. If the garter remained in position, the omens were good; if it fell down, then she would not have the children she wished. Her future husband had not to know anything about this charm, otherwise it would not work. In fastening the garter around the leg, she had to quote a certain verse, but no-one seems to know the words.

Friday is known as POETS Day by those who work from Monday to Friday. The initial letters mean: Push Off Early, Tomorrow's Saturday!

Saturday

A child born on Saturday works hard for a living; it's a bad day for cutting hair and nails and for getting married because it brings misfortune, and no self-respecting housewife washed the clothes on a Saturday. There is an old Yorkshire belief that the sun always shines on a Saturday, if only for a few moments, but a new moon on a Saturday heralds bad weather, bad fortune, storms at sea and general bad luck. To sneeze on a Saturday means you will see your lover the following day.

JANUARY

"As the days do lengthen, so the cold does strengthen"

January has not always been the beginning of the legal year in England. It once began on Lady Day (25 March) but since the calendar changes of 1752, the official year has begun on 1 January.

In BC 713, the Roman Emperor Numa instituted a feast on the first of January. It was dedicated to Janus, god of the new year who kept the gates of heaven. He is honoured as a guardian of doors and gates and is depicted with two faces, one looking backwards and the other forwards.

In Anglo-Saxon times, we knew January as Wolfmonath, the month of the hungry wolf because wolves were troublesome through a shortage of food. January has also been called Se aeftera geola (the after-Yule) and forma monath, meaning the first month.

Days in January

1 January — New Year's Day

It is vital to start the New Year by having a Lucky Bird (pronounced bod in parts of Yorkshire) as the first visitor to one's home. He is also known as First Foot, but he must be male; he must have dark hair, he must not be flat footed and his eye brows should not meet in the middle. He must carry into the house certain items which guarantee good fortune. These vary but can include a sprig of evergreen like holly, a piece of coal, a portion of bread, some money and a pinch of salt, these symbolising the necessities of life while the evergreen signifies continuing life.

Inside, he must place a gift on the hearth and will be given a drink and perhaps a piece of ginger cake. The custom varies across the county; in parts, bachelors are essential and further north, they must be fair haired. Early on New Year's morning, Yorkshire children would go around the houses shouting this verse:

> "Lucky-bod, lucky bod, chuck, chuck, chuck,
> Maister an' missus, it's tahme ti git up;
> If thoo dissn't git up, thoo'll have neea luck,
> Lucky bod, lucky bod, chuck, chuck, chuck."

13

It was hoped this would produce small gifts of money or sweets and another Yorkshire saying for New Year's Day is that:

"At New Year's tide, days lengthen a cock-stride."

This means that the days lengthen imperceptibly — a cock-stride is a very short day. There is also a Yorkshire belief that the weather on the first three days of January rules the coming three months, while another saying for 1 January goes:

"Morning red, foul weather and great need ahead."

In some parts of Yorkshire, apple trees were wassailed on 1 January. This entailed singing, dancing, feasting and drinking with ale being dashed upon the trees to ensure a good crop. A wassail bowl, or vessel bowl, of hot liquor was passed around with an apple floating in it. The word 'wassail' comes from the Anglo-Saxon *wes hal* meaning "be of good health" and this custom varied across the country, both in its form and in its date. Wassailing was sometimes held in the autumn, or during Advent, or at Christmas and even on the feast of the Epiphany (6 January).

In Yorkshire and other parts of the north, the following verse might be sung when the wassail bowl was carried around:

"Here we come a-wassailing among the leaves so green,
Here we come a-wandering, so fair to be seen.
Love and joy come to you, and to your wassail too,
And God bless you, and send you, a Happy New Year."

Other events on 1 January included the baking and selling of God Cakes, small pies filled with mincemeat. At Driffield, children would scramble for coins which had been heated on a shovel and thrown into the air. The crowd chanted,

"'Ere we are at oor toon end,
A shoulder o' mutton an' a crown ti spend."

At Hutton Conyers near Ripon, shepherds held a meal of frummety, apple pies and cake to mark the allocation of sheep grazing rights by the manorial court.

5 January — Eve of Twelfth Night; Old Christmas Eve; Eve of the Epiphany

Depending when you start to count, this can be regarded as Twelfth Night. In parts of Yorkshire, it is the day for taking down the Christmas decorations which, in some cases, used to consist of horse shoes bearing twelve nails, one for each of the twelve days. Wassailing used to occur and bonfires were lit.

6 January — The Feast of the Epiphany; Twelfth Day

This is the twelfth day after Christmas when the infant Christ was revealed to the world by the visit of the Three Wise Kings. The word 'epiphany' means manifestation or apparition.

It was an apple wassailing day. Christmas decorations must be removed otherwise bad luck will befall the household, whilst just across the Yorkshire border at Brough, a burning holly tree was carried through the town. As the tree burned, youths tried to seize a blazing twig and carry it to a pub — the successful ones were rewarded with free beer. The purpose and origin of this custom has been lost!

Once the most festive of the Twelve Days of Christmas in the north of England, there is a belief that an east wind on this day brings full baskets of fruit in the autumn.

7 January — St. Distaff's Day; Rock Day

There is no saint called Distaff, the name being jokingly applied to the distaff which is a cleft stick used by spinners to hold the yarn or flax. The use of a distaff in spinning was introduced to this country in 1505. Rock is another name for a distaff. On St. Distaff's Day, the day after Twelfth Night, the women spinners of Yorkshire returned to work after Christmas. There was some fun too — the men burned the flax and tow used by the women, and the women drenched the men with water. In some areas, these celebrations were moved to Plough Monday (see later). An old saying goes:

"Partly work and partly play, ye must on St. Distaff's Day."

13 January — St. Hilary's Day

St. Hilary (AD315-367) was made a doctor of the church in 1851 and in England, has given his name to the Hilary Term; this marks the beginning of the legal and university terms each new year.

In Yorkshire and elsewhere, St. Hilary's Day is said to be the coldest of the year. This follows a severe frost in 1205 which started on 13 January and continued until 22 March. In places, this was the first day after Christmas upon which weddings could be conducted.

18 January — Old Twelfth Day

This marks the traditional end of the apple wassailing season.

20 January — St. Agnes' Eve

The day before St. Agnes' Day, Yorkshire lasses would fast and never speak while hoping to foresee their future. In particular, they yearned the identity of their future sweethearts or husbands. During this day, they made Dumb Cakes, charms which would induce visions; at night, having fasted all day without speaking, they would eat the cakes then walk backwards upstairs to bed. Before going to sleep, and in the hope of dreaming of their lover, they would chant:

> "Fair St. Agnes, play thy part
> And send to me my own sweetheart,
> Not in his best nor worst array,
> But in his apparel for every day.
> That I tomorrow may him ken
> From among all other men."

A variation of this occurred at Lastingham in the North York Moors. Young women would visit St. Cedd's Well and perform the ceremony of washing their garters.

This was a sign that they would remain virgins until they met the right man; sometimes, they would unravel a piece of woollen stocking and knit it into a small item to be worn by their true love when his identity became known.

At nearby Rosedale, a maid had to visit the churchyard at midnight, pick a blade of grass from a bachelor's grave, then walk home backwards to bed. She must undress by removing her clothes in exactly the same sequence as she had put them on and put the grass under her pillow. Then she would dream of her lover! For those who could not perform these rituals today, they could be done any Friday except Good Friday.

21 January — St. Agnes' Day; Sheep Blessing Day

Churches in the sheep farming districts hold services at which the flocks are blessed. Sometimes, a lamb is symbolically decorated and led into the church as part of a procession. The emblem of St. Agnes is a lamb, signifying her innocence as a young girl, thus many sheep blessing services were held this day. Now, they are held on the nearest Sunday.

22 January — St. Vincent's Day

The Yorkshire weather prognostication for this day is:

> "If the sun shines on St. Vincent's Day, there will be much wind."

25 January — The Conversion of St. Paul; St. Ananias' Day; Burns Night

Many mistakenly believe this is St. Paul's feast day, but it is not; that occurs on 29 June, a day he shares with St. Peter. Today honours Paul's famous conversion on the road to Damascus; it was Ananias who restored his sight that day.

It is important for weather prognostication, an old verse saying:

> "If St. Paul's be fair and clear,
> It doth betide a happy year,
> But if by chance it then should rain,
> It will make dear all kinds of grain.
> And if the clouds make dark the sky,
> Then cattle and fowls this year will die;
> If blustering winds do blow aloft,
> Then wars shall trouble the kingdom oft."

The Scots poet, Robbie Burns (1759-1796) is honoured in nationwide celebrations this night.

26 January — Lost Trawlermen's Day; Australia Day

On the Sunday nearest 26 January, a wreath-laying ceremony occurs on St. Andrew's Dock at Hull to honour trawlermen from the city who have lost their lives. In the last forty years, ninety-nine trawlermen from Hull have been lost on 26 January — 40 were lost on 26 January in 1955; one was lost on this date in 1965 and 58 were lost on 26 January 1968. Many have perished on other dates too. It is hoped the Lost Trawlermen's Day will remind others of their sacrifice. Sir Francis Drake also died this day in 1596.

Another sea-faring link is that Yorkshire navigator, Captain James Cook (1728-1779) of Marton and Great Ayton discovered Australia in 1770 and this day celebrates his achievement. He sailed from Whitby in the locally built *Endeavour*.

Miscellaneous days in January

Hansel Monday; Land Letting Day. On the first Monday in the New

Year, it was customary in the north to give children and household servants a present. This was transferred to Boxing Day but now seems obsolete in favour of Christmas. The gifts were taken into the house by the First Foot on New Year's Day and are called handsel.

A candle auction is held at The George Inn, Hubberholme in Wharfedale where 16 acres of land at Poor Pasture is auctioned for the benefit of the needy. Pensioners now receive coal from the proceeds. The custom is probably 400 years old and bidders must complete the auction before a candle finishes burning. During the year, a candle is always alight in the bar of the inn during licensing hours.

Plough Sunday — see Plough Monday

Plough Monday. This is the first Monday after the Epiphany (6 January), when farm labourers returned to work after Christmas. (See 7 January). In some areas, ploughs are blessed in church today or the nearest Sunday (Plough Sunday), and one custom was for a team of lads to haul a plough from door to door and ask for money against a threat of ploughing the garden path!

A variation continues at Goathland when all-male Plough Stots perform their splendid sword dance around the village, but not until the Saturday after Plough Sunday. A similar team operates at Knaresborough on Plough Sunday and in 1986, the custom was revived at Bolton Percy. Also on Plough Monday, curd tarts were begged by plough lads at Slingsby, Muker and Redmire.

FEBRUARY

"Rain in February is worth as much as manure."

February, our shortest month, was known to the Anglo-Saxons as Sprout Kale because cabbages and kale sprouted. This month and January were added to the calendar around 700 BC, January at the beginning of the year with February at the end. February is named after an ancient Roman festival, Februa, itself presided over by the god Februus. That festival involved purification ceremonies, examples of which still occur on Candlemas Day. The decimvirs placed February next to January in BC 452 where it has remained. Many of us know it as February Fill-Dyke because of its heavy rain.

There is a Yorkshire saying which goes:

"February fill-dyke — fill it wi' either black or white;
March muck it oot wi' a besom an' a cloot."

Black and white here means rain or snow. Other sayings about February include:

"There's allus yar fair week in February."
"February fire lang, March tide to bed gang;"
"Warm February, bad hay crop; Cawd February, good hay crop."

Days in February

1 February — The Calends of February, St. Bride's Day; the Eve of Candlemas

Interest on debts fell due on the Calends of February and proclamations were made. St. Bridget, who is also known as St. Bride, was nicknamed the White Goddess of England, Scotland and Ireland. In parts of Yorkshire, Christmas decorations were removed and it is the day for eating oat cakes.

2 February — The Feast of the Purification of the Blessed Virgin Mary; Candlemas Day; Wives' Feast Day; Cradle Rocking Day; Groundhog Day

A most important day in the Yorkshire rural calendar, this is rich with weather lore. The best known, written in differing forms, goes:

19

"If Candlemas be fair and bright, Winter will have another flight;

If Candlemas be cloudy with rain, Winter will not come again."

In Yorkshire, this verse emerges as:

"If Can'lemas be lound an' fair, Ya Hauf o' t'winter's ti cum an' mair.

If Can'lemas day be murk an' foul, Ya hauf o' t'winter's geean at Yule."

Yorkshire farmers reckon it's wise to have half one's store of animal fodder left at Candlemas, just in case the weather turns worse. "Allus have half thy fodder left at Candlemas" is the wisdom. Another verse reads like this:

"In Yorkshire, ancient people say,
If February's second day
Be very fair and clear
It doth portend a scanty year,
For hay and grass, but if it rains,
They never then perplex their brains."

By Candlemas the nights are growing lighter and it was, by tradition, the time to put away one's household candles. Yorkshire folk would say:

"On Can'lemas, a February day, Throw t' can'le an' can'lestick away."

Another saying, strong among the Yorkshire fishing communities, goes:

"A Can'lemas crack lays monny a sailor on his back."

Apart from weather and candles away, Candlemas Day remains important for Yorkshire gardeners. It is a planting day — peas, lettuce, sweet peas, onions, beans and cabbages should be planted as this advice reminds us,

"On Candlemas Day, stick your beans in the clay
Throw candle and candlestick right away."

It is also the day that Yorkshire geese would start to lay their eggs — "At Can'lemas, good geese l' lay."

Ancient Yorkshire tradition also says the snowdrop blooms on this day. Known as the Purification Flower or the Fair Maid of

20

February, snowdrops were gathered by maidens and worn in honour of Our Lady as a symbol of purity. A candlelit ceremony was held in church and wives would also hold a feast on this day in honour of the Virgin Mary and so it was known as Wives' Feast Day. In some areas, fairs were held, Pontefract being one example.

Today is Cradle Rocking Day at Blidworth in Nottinghamshire. The last male child born in the parish is placed in a wooden cradle within the church and rocked twelve times before the altar. This represents the child Jesus in the Temple. The actual service is held on the first Sunday of February. It is also Groundhog Day in America, a Quarter Day in Scotland when rents are due, and in legal terms it was a Not Day, i.e. *dies non*, a day when no legal business was conducted.

3 February — St. Blaise's Day; Throat Blessing Day; Sheriff Pricking Day

In the wool districts of Yorkshire, especially Bradford, St. Blaise processions were held because he is the patron saint of woolcombers. Popular in the 18th and 19th centuries, they ended as the industry declined. There is a statue of St. Blaise at the Wool Exchange in Bradford and several Yorkshire inns are named in his honour. Because St. Blaise had an ability to cure disease of the throat, this day was also Throat Blessing Day.

Yorkshire continues with the office of sheriff and it is Sheriff Pricking Day. The Sovereign makes the final selection by using a silver bodkin to prick a parchment bearing their names. (See 12 November).

4 February — St. Gilbert of Sempringham's Day

Sempringham is in Lincolnshire but North Yorkshire boasted a fine Gilbertine Priory. St. Gilbert (1085-1189) founded the only true English order of monks, albeit under the Rule of St. Benedict. Gilbert was over a hundred years old when he died in 1189, being canonised by the Pope in 1202, but his Gilbertine Order, which had expanded to 20 monasteries, was suppressed by Henry VIII at the Reformation. The remains of the priory are at Old Malton; it is no longer Catholic and forms part of St. Mary's Anglican church.

6 February — Accession Day

Loyal Yorkshire folk remember the accession to the throne of our present Queen, Elizabeth II, on 6 February 1952. Her Coronation Day was 2 June 1953.

7 February — St. Romuald's Day

St. Romuald died around AD 950 and may have given his name to Romaldkirk on the Yorkshire banks of the River Tees. This village was transferred to County Durham as a result of the 1974 boundary changes. Another theory is that St. Romald (not Romuald) was the son of a Northumbrian prince and it was he who gave his name to this village. The splendid parish church is known as The Cathedral of the Dales.

10 February — Umbrella Day

The day when English people carry an umbrella to mark the invention of this article. No self-respecting Yorkshireman would be seen celebrating. As one said, "Umbrellas is mighty rare contraptions on t' Yorkshire moors."

14 February — St. Valentine's Day; Plum Shuttle Eating Day

There are some 52 saints valled Valentine and two share this day. Neither was a Yorkshireman. Nonetheless, in Yorkshire as elsewhere, the day is full of romance which dates from ancient times when maidens lovingly made decorated messages and placed them in a large urn. Along came hopeful young men to withdraw a message at random, rather like tombola.

When a youth selected a girl, she would accompany him at public events for the remainder of the year. The church approved the custom by transferring it to St. Valentine's Day, and so the romantic occasion was instituted. Valentine was not romantic; indeed, he was a priest who, when jailed, sent a note to the pretty daughter of his captor, thanking her for her friendship. He signed the note, "Your Valentine". Now, romantic people send anonymous cards to each other in the hope it will produce everlasting love.

One old Yorkshire custom was for a lovesick girl to take a hard boiled egg, remove the yolk and fill the cavity with salt. Before going to bed, she would eat the egg, after which she must neither talk nor drink. Having undergone this ritual, she believed she would dream of the man she would marry.

St. Valentine's Day is when the birds are said to mate, and when crops are sown, often from hoppers or seed baskets — the saying goes:

"St. Valentine, set thy hopper by mine."

Many Yorkshiremen would ensure their beans were sown no later than St. Valentine's Day.

"On St. Valentine's Day, beans should be in the clay."

A further piece of advice when sowing beans was to plant four for every one expected to reach maturity:

"One to rot and one to grow,
One for the pigeon and one for the crow!"

It is believed in parts of Yorkshire that the crocus, a flower dedicated to this saint, blooms on St. Valentine's Day. Further afield, it is Plum Shuttle Eating Day; these are dough buns shaped like shuttles and made with caraway seeds and currants. Signen cake is eaten in Cumberland and fishing nets are blessed in Northumberland.

29 February — Leap Year Day; Backward Bean Day

This day occurs once every four years, during leap year. It is officially either an Intercalary Day or a Bissextile Day — the latter name means that, legally, the day is two days! This is one of several devices to make the year correct in its duration. In the Roman calendar, 24 February appeared twice for this reason, thus producing 23, 24, 24 and then 25 February, and in this country, through a law passed by Henry III in 1175, the Bissextile Day and the day preceding it were classified as a single day. Later, the extra day was moved to 29 February.

Its purpose is to ensure the years are of equal duration at least once every four years! The idea came from Julius Caesar. He knew that each year was five hours, 48 minutes and 46 seconds too long which, over a long period, threw the seasons into chaos. His astronomers introduced the extra day to balance the timetable and it has been included ever since.

By ancient tradition, girls are allowed to propose to boys on 29 February; this began when St. Bridget complained to St. Patrick that women should be able to propose marriage, upon which he said it could occur only on 29 February! Bridget promptly proposed to him but he rejected her for the church, and presented her with a fine silk gown as compensation.

For a time, it was said that any woman proposing marriage to a man on this day had to wear a red petticoat, part of which must show beneath her dress; it was this custom which led to the term 'a scarlet woman'.

Yorkshire people believe that anything started on 29 February will be successful, and it is a particularly good day to be born. Getting married in a Leap Year is also considered wise:

> "Happy them'll be that wed and wive
> Within a leap year — they're sure to thrive."

It is also considered a good day to begin a long journey — in older times, travellers were given forget-me-knots as they departed. One exception to these rules is the sowing of beans — an old Yorkshireman said to me, "Nivver sow beans on 29 February — if thoo dis, they'll grow backwards in their pods!" Hence it is known as Backward Bean Day.

Miscellaneous days in February

Because Easter is a moveable feast, the days of Lent are also variable and some of the following may arrive in either February or March. It is rare for any of these days to arrive on Leap Year Day, 29 February; I believe, for example, that Shrove Tuesday fell on 29 February in 1876 but never since. Another rarity is for five Sundays to fall in February. This occurred in 1976 and I believe the previous occasion was 1824.

Septuagesima Sunday — The third Sunday before Lent, so called because, in round figures, there are 70 days to go before Easter. In fact, there are nine weeks.

Sexagesima Sunday — The second Sunday before Lent, so called because, in round figures, there are 60 days before Easter. In fact, there are eight weeks.

Egg Saturday, Quinquagesima Eve; Brusting Sunday — The last Saturday before Lent when Oxford students are given hardboiled, decorated eggs. Brusting pudding is a type of pancake eaten in

Lincolnshire today. In Yorkshire, brusten or brussen means to over indulge in food — e.g. "Ah's fair brussen". A Yorkshire person who regularly ate too much was known as brussenkite.

Quinquagesima Sunday; Shrove Sunday — The Sunday before Lent, so called because there are about 50 days before Easter. Because this is the last Sunday before Lent, it was the final time for feasting before the Lenten fast. It is followed by Collop Monday, Shrove Tuesday and Ash Wednesday which is the first day of Lent.

Collop Monday; Blue Monday; Nickanan Night; Dappy Door Night; Lent Sherd Night — Collops are eaten in Yorkshire households today. A collop is a large piece of meat, such as ham or bacon, and it is fried with eggs, potatoes, tomatoes, mushrooms, liver — and virtually anything else. The idea is feast heavily before the Lenten fast — and this is also the last opportunity to finish off the good food because, in every Yorkshire household, nowt is wasted.

The day was also known as Blue Monday because some drank to excess before Lent; it was Nickanan Night when youths hid gates or knocked on doors and ran away. Another name was Dappy Door Night or Lent Sherd Night when children tapped on doors hoping for a gift of sweets. These were the forerunner of our modern Mischief Night (4 November) and Trick-or-Treat Night (31 October).

Shrove Tuesday; Pancake Tuesday; Kepping Day; Egg Shackling Day; Hurling Day; Bonny Ball Day; Dog Tossing Day; Cock Throwing Day; Cock Fighting Day; Lent Crocking Day; Crockery Smashing Day; Barring Out Day — The name Shrove Tuesday is from the Catholic custom of confessing sins before Lent. The old word was to shrive; when the confession was complete, the person was shriven or they had been shrove. Hence the name of Shrove Tuesday.

Pancakes were eaten to use up the left-over goodies — eggs, butter, fat and so forth. It was the final luxury before the Lenten fast. The first three pancakes were set aside — "One for St. Peter, one for St. Paul, and one for Him who made us all!" Pancake races, where the competitors run a course while tossing pancakes from frying pans, are popular throughout Yorkshire and some are heralded by the ringing of the Pancake Bell. At York, journeymen and their apprentices were allowed to enter York Minster and ring the bell. The doors were left open for them.

At Scarborough there is a curious skipping display. When the Pancake Bell sounds, school children from Scarborough begin to skip on the seafront and continue for five hours. The custom may have started when children of fishermen helped their fathers untangle fishing lines — and then used them as makeshift skipping ropes. Scarborough's Pancake Bell was originally in the Hospital of St. Thomas the Martyr but is now in the Rotunda Museum. Pancake Bells are sounded in other Yorkshire towns including Bingley and Richmond. In some areas, poor children would beg for pancakes —this was known as Lent Crocking.

Shrove Tuesday was known as Kepping Day in the East Riding; coloured balls were thrown about and the people had to catch (kep) them.

A type of football is played on Shrove Tuesday but bears little resemblance to soccer. It consists of teams of local youths from rival communities kicking balls along the streets towards specified places. It is played at Sedgefield in Co. Durham.

Shrove Tuesday is also known as Egg Shackling Day (when eggs bearing the name of children are placed in a sack and shaken gently. As the shells crack, the eggs are removed. The child whose name is on the last egg to survive receives a prize). Hurling Day is when a game like rugby football, called hurling, is played. The ball is wooden and the teams comprise up to 500 members. It is also Bonny Ball Day in some areas when coloured balls of wool are bounced up and down on a string, while on Crockery Smashing Day, crockery was smashed outside houses to ensure the householders gave pancakes to the smashers.

Barring Out Day was when children in the West Riding would bar teachers from entering school until they consented to a holiday. When the holiday was agreed, ginger parkin was eaten in celebration.

The day has also been called Dog Tossing Day, Cock Fighting Day and Cock Throwing Day, all these now being illegal.

In Wensleydale, the blowing of the Bainbridge Horn ceases until 28 September.

Ash Wednesday, Hash Wednesday, Fruttace Wednesday — This is the first day of Lent. In the sixth century, Pope Gregory the Great began the custom of sprinkling ashes on the heads of the faithful as a sign of penitence. The custom continues in Catholic churches throughout Yorkshire, when small ashen crosses are marked on the foreheads of the congregation. Nothing white should be worn.

In parts of the Dales, it was called Fruttace Wednesday because fritters, or fruttaces made from flour, eggs, apples, dried fruit and spice were eaten. Tutt-Ball, a game like rounders, was played in the Holderness area of the East Riding. In some places, it was called Hash Wednesday; this is not an error for Ash, but to indicate that a hash, a quick meal, was concocted from the previous days' left-overs.

Fritter Thursday; Bloody Thursday — The day following Fruttace Wednesday when more fritters or fruttaces were eaten in the Dales and Moors. It was known as Bloody Thursday in the Cleveland Hills because black puddings were eaten.

Kissing Day — The Friday following Shrove Tuesday was a day when every Yorkshire lad had the right to kiss any girl — but only once. The custom is thought to have survived since Viking times.

Quadragesima Sunday — The first Sunday in Lent, the 40th day before Easter.

Ember Days — The Wednesday, Friday and Saturday after the first Sunday in Lent, days of fasting and prayer.

MARCH

"A peck of March dust is worth a King's ransom."

Once the first month, March was placed third when January and February were introduced around 700 BC. It is named after Mars, the god of war and in Anglo-Saxon times was called Hreth-monath or Hyldmonath, the rough month, due to its powerful winds. It was also Hlydmonath, the stormy or windy month. It was later referred to as Lenctenmonath, the month of lengthening days.

Yorkshire country people describe March as "T' month of monny weathers" due to its wide-ranging moods. It is also said that March has borrowed three days from the end of February because, quite often, the first days of March are very wintry. One old saying is:

"A dry March, a wet April and a cool May,
Fills barns, cellars and brings much hay."

From the West Riding comes this saying:

"A dry March, an' a windy,
A full barn, an' a findy."

More generally, it is said "For every fog i' March, there'll be a frost i' May", but perhaps the best known saying is that "If March comes in like a lion, it will go out like a lamb, but if it comes in like a lamb, then it will go out like a lion." Lion and lamb represent the extremes of the month's weather patterns. At Whitby, this old verse was often quoted: "March grows, nivver dows." It means that plants which grow in March will never thrive.

Days in March

1 March — St. David's Day; Whuppity Scoorie Day

Leeks are worn by patriotic Welsh people to honour St. David's patronage of their country, and there is a pea and bean-sowing link with Yorkshire:

"Sow peas and beans on David or Chad."

This is an exhortation to plant one's new peas and beans by no later than tomorrow, St. Chad's Day. Oats and Barley should also be planted.

In Lanarkshire, Whuppity Scoorie Day is an ancient ceremony for chasing away the winter.

2 March — St. Chad's Day

St. Chad was abbot of a monastery at Lastingham in the North York Moors. It was founded by his brother, Cedd who died after attending the Synod of Whitby in AD 664. Cedd is also a saint. Chad gained an immense reputation for holiness becoming Bishop of Lichfield and patron of many Midlands churches. At Lastingham there is a wonderful apsidal crypt dating 1078 which is beneath the church of St. Mary. It is the only surviving Norman crypt with a chancel, nave and two side aisles. St. Cedd's grave is said to lie beneath this crypt, whilst the Catholic cathedral in Birmingham contains some relics of St. Chad.

Yorkshire farmers would expect their geese to begin laying eggs by this date — "Before St. Chad, every goose lays, whether good or bad!"

3 March — St. Aelred's Day

St. Aelred was a famous Abbot of Rievaulx near Helmsley. Today, the abbey ruins are among the most visited in England and it was Aelred who coined a very apt phrase about its location. He said, "It provides a marvellous freedom from the tumult of the world."

8 March — National No-Smoking Day

In 1989, this was declared the first National No-Smoking Day, the purpose being to persuade those who smoked cigarettes, cigars and pipes to abandon their habit. Its effect upon Yorkshire folk has never been determined.

12 March — St. Gregory's Day; Farmers' Day; Gregory-Great-Onion Day

This is when northern farmers celebrate their status. In addition, both Lancastrians and Yorkshire folk in the Pennines referred to it as Gregory-Great-Onion Day because it was an excellent time to sow onions.

St. Gregory was Pope Gregory the Great (c.540-604), patron saint of scholars. He sent St. Augustine to Canterbury to convert the English after fair-haired Angles were sold as slaves in Rome. He said they were angels and told Augustine to convert those who were so cruel to innocent children. Along with some 30 other churches, the ancient Kirkdale Minster near Kirkbymoorside is dedicated to St. Gregory. Its Saxon sundial is the most complete in the world and the church bears the longest inscription known to have survived since Anglo-Saxon times.

17 March — St. Patrick's Day

Some Yorkshire gardeners insist on planting their potatoes no later than St. Patrick's Day, while others insist that Good Friday is the crucial date. As St. Patrick is the patron saint of Ireland, the Irish also plant their potatoes today.

19 March — St. Joseph's Day

This St. Joseph was the husband of the Virgin Mary, and an old country saying, once prevalent throughout Yorkshire, is that: "If St. Joseph's be clear, so follows a fertile year." It is a good day to marry.

20 March — St. Cuthbert's Day

Crayke, a tiny hilltop village north of York, will forever be associated with St. Cuthbert. When Cuthbert died on this day in AD 687, he was buried on the Farne Islands but during the Viking raids, the monks, fearing desecration of his remains, fled with his body. For the next seven years, they toured the north of England with Cuthbert's remains; the body had not decomposed and eventually they settled in Chester-le-Street, Co. Durham. A century later, new threats from maurauding Danes caused another flight. This time, the monks brought Cuthbert's body to Yorkshire. They rested at Ripon, but his body was concealed for four months at Crayke. By tradition, every place his body rested became a part of County Durham and so Crayke, in the North Riding of Yorkshire, belonged to the County Palatine of Durham until 1844. An Act of Parliament restored it to Yorkshire.

Oddly enough, two years before Cuthbert's death, he was given land at Crayke where he founded a monastery.

That monastery became St. Cuthbert's church and thus Crayke church is dedicated to its founder and not its patron.

Crayke hill is reputed to be the location of the nursery rhyme which says the Grand Old Duke of York had ten thousand men and marched them up to the top of the hill and marched them down again.

21 March — The spring equinox

This day is important for fixing the date of Easter. Easter Day falls on the Sunday following the 14th day of the calendar moon which happens on or next after 21 March. The method of determining the method for fixing the date of Easter was decided at Whitby Abbey (see later).

This used to be St. Benedict's Day when, according to Yorkshire gardeners, peas should be sown; failure to plant them by today meant the crop would fail. St. Benedict's Day has been moved to 11 July.

25 March — Lady Day; St. Mary's Day in Lent

Until 1752, this was the beginning of the English legal year and New Year's Day. The day's full title is "The Feast of the Annunciation of Our Lady, the Blessed Virgin Mary". To distinguish it from other days dedicated to Our Lady, it was known as "St. Mary's Day in Lent" and later by the simple title of Lady Day. Landlords required payment of rent by their tenants and new tenancies, or terminations of tenancies, were conducted from this date.

Due to a prophecy by Mother Shipton of Knaresborough, there was a widespread belief that if either Good Friday or Easter Day fall on Lady Day, then some national misfortune will befall this country in the following year. The saying is:

"If Our Lord falls into Our Lady's lap,
England will meet with a great mishap."

Two examples are quoted: In 1910, when Good Friday fell on 25 March, King Edward VII died the following May. In 1951, Easter Sunday fell on 25 March, and King George VI died less than eleven months later, on 6 February 1952. See 5 April and 2 July.

28 March — St. Alkelda's Day

Only two churches in Yorkshire, and probably the whole of England are named after St. Alkelda. They are at Middleham and Giggleswick. Legend says that Alkelda was a Saxon princess murdered by Viking women and buried at Middleham. St. Alkelda's famous Ebbing and Flowing well is near Giggleswick. In Yorkshire, the old name for a well is keld, and the Anglo-Saxon word for holy was halig. A holy well was Haligkeld, or Hallikeld; it is suggested that Alkelda is the name of a holy well and not a person.

29, 30 and 31 March — Borrowing Days

The last three days of March are borrowed from April — a saying adds "March borrows three days of April, and they are ill."

In Yorkshire, the following verse is applied to this:

"March borrowed frev April,
Three days and they were ill;
T' fost of 'em was wind and weet,
T' second was nowt but snow and sleet,
And t' thod was sike an awful freeze
That t' poor bods' legs was stuck ti t' trees."

Miscellaneous Days in March

Kiplingcotes Derby Day — The third Thursday of March witnesses the Kiplingcotes Derby, the oldest "flat" race in England. It is far from flat because the course traverses ploughed fields, ditches and the main A163 road, and climbs some 300 feet to the finishing post. It has been held annually since 1519 at Kiplingcotes on the Yorkshire Wolds near Market Weighton, and is run over a testing four-and-a-half mile course. Men and women may compete, provided they weigh *more* than 10 stone but they can make up their weight with heavy objects. The winner receives a trophy and a cash prize from a legacy invested in 1618 — worth less than £10, while the person who comes second receives all the stake money. Twenty runners at £4.25 per head entry fee makes a good second prize!

Ted, Mid, Miserae, Carlin, Palm and Pace Egg Day — These are names for Sundays in Lent. In the Cleveland Hills, Pace Egg Day was called Good Feast Day, but the sequence does not allow for a fifth Sunday, ie between Carlin and Palm. The first three names come from the Latin Mass and are based on Te Deum, Mi Deus and Miserere mei. Carlin Sunday and Palm Sunday follow, while Pace Egg Day is another name for Easter Sunday. Pace Eggs were rolled down Yorkshire hillsides.

Carlin Sunday; Carr Sunday, Care Sunday, Mothering Sunday, Refreshment Sunday, Simnel Sunday — This is the fourth Sunday in Lent although, in bygone times, the fifth Sunday of Lent was Care or Carr Sunday, ie the day before Palm Sunday. Even now, Carlin Sunday is celebrated on the fifth Sunday of Lent (Passion Sunday) in some districts.

Yorkshire claims the origin of Carlin Sunday. A village, Carlin How, on the north-east coast of Yorkshire was starving when a ship went ashore during a storm. Its cargo was small grey or brown peas. The villagers raided the wreck and survived the famine by eating those peas. That day has been commemorated ever since as Carlin Sunday but Carlin How lies in Cleveland County. It was part of the North Riding until 1974.

Throughout Yorkshire and the north east of England, carlin peas are still eaten on Carlin Sunday; after being steeped in water, they are fried in butter and seasoned, usually with salt and pepper. Several northern pubs serve them. It is more likely, however, that the name comes from care or carr, meaning penance, and that the eating of these peas was a penance prior to the Lenten fast.

It was also the custom today for young people working away to return to visit their mothers.

"On Mothering Sunday above all other,
Every child should dine with its mother."

The youngsters took bunches of violets, the emblem for today, and when they arrived home they were given simnel cakes. Because they ate with mother, it was known as Refreshment Sunday, and because simnel cakes were eaten, it was called Simnel Sunday. The centuries-old Mothering Sunday should not be confused with Mother's Day which is an American invention dating from 1911 and occurring on the second Sunday in May.

Passion Sunday — The fifth Sunday of Lent. Dock Pudding, known as Passion Dock, is a concoction of dock leaves, onions, nettles and oatmeal. It is eaten in parts of Yorkshire today. The first Dock Pudding Championship was held at Hebden Bridge in 1971. Carlin Peas are sometimes eaten today (see Carlin Sunday).

Palm Sunday; Palm Cross Day, Spanish Sunday, Fig Sunday —The last Sunday of Lent, ie the Sunday before Easter, and a good day for Yorkshire gardeners to sow flower seeds. It is known as Fig Sunday because figs were eaten in parts of Yorkshire and Spanish Sunday because a drink made from liquorice and water was consumed. The name Palm Cross comes from the custom of fashioning crosses from palm leaves; these were, and still are, distributed in some Yorkshire churches, chiefly Catholic ones. Pussy willow, the flowers of the goat willow, are sometimes substituted. Palmsun Fairs were held in Stokesley and Guisborough and Fieldkirk Fair was held near Morley. An old verse goes:

"Palm Sunday, palm away,
Next Sunday's Easter Day."

Maundy Thursday; Chare or Shere Thursday — The day before Good Friday. Named from the first words of the antiphon of the day *Mandatum novum do vobis* (A new commandment I give you), this being used in the ancient ceremony of washing the feet once carried out in Catholic churches and monasteries. Kings, prelates and priests all washed the feet of the poor. The name is erroneously thought to come from *maund*, a basket, because in some areas food was distributed to the poor. Today, the Sovereign distributes Maundy Money, the number of recipients corresponding to the age of the Sovereign. In addition to its base in London's Westminster Abbey, the ceremony has been conducted in Yorkshire churches, namely Selby Abbey (1969), York Minster (1972) and Ripon Cathedral (1985). The very first "Maundy" of clothing and food costing £4.13s.9d. was given to the poor by King John in 1210 at Knaresborough, three years before the first Maundy Money ceremony at Rochester in 1213.

Chare or Shere Thursday may be linked to the custom of cleaning the altars in readiness for Easter.

Good Friday; Parsley Planting Day, Tatie Planting Day — The Friday before Easter, commemorating the Crucifixion. The word 'good' means holy. Marble championships, started in 1600 were contested for the hand of a fair maiden and modern versions are held today, including a Marbles Championship near Crawley, West Sussex. It is a busy day for gardeners — in Yorkshire, potaoes are planted and in some areas it is a parsley planting day, the parsley being placed in the earth at the hour of the crucifixion.

In some places, it is the day for spraying fruit trees with insecticides.

There is a widespread belief that anything planted on Good Friday will thrive. This stems from an ancient notion that the Devil was powerless on this holy day and unable to harm the seeds. Blacksmiths did not work because one of them had made the nails used at the Crucifixion and one very old Yorkshire practice was never to disturb the soil on Good Friday with anything made from iron. Wooden tools had to be used but that custom ended long ago. Yorkshire farmers said,

> "On Good Friday, rist they pleeaf;
> Start nowt, end nowt, that's eneeaf!"

A Pace Egg play is performed at Sowerby Bridge and in parts of Yorkshire, special Easter biscuits are made. Hot Cross Buns are also a traditional food, an old saying being: "Hot Cross Buns, Hot Cross Buns, one a penny, two a penny, Hot Cross Buns." Bread made today and marked with a cross was thought never to go mouldy and loaves were hung in the rafters, often surviving for years.

Easter Sunday; Easter Day; Pace Egg Day; Troll Egg Day; Buckle Snatching Day; Egg Jauping Day — A Yorkshireman once told me, "Easter Sunday is the first Sunday after the first full moon after you've planted your onions". He was probably right, but the official method was determined in Yorkshire at Whitby Abbey in AD 664. That method is still used. Easter falls on the first Sunday after the full moon which happens on or next after the twenty-first day of March, and if the full moon happens on a Sunday, then Easter Day is the Sunday after. Thus, Easter Sunday can never fall earlier than 22 March nor later than 25 April.

Prior to AD 664, the Celtic branch of the church in the north celebrated Easter on a date which differed from that used by Christians in the south; King Oswy of Northumbria, whose kingdom embraced Yorkshire, wanted everyone to celebrate Easter together and so the matter was discussed at the Synod of Whitby. After a lot of argument, St. Wilfred of Ripon (see 12 October) reminded the gathering that St. Peter and his successors in Rome held the keys to the Kingdom of Heaven and recommended the Roman method of calculation. This was agreed and so it has been ever since. The Vatican favours a fixed Easter — if other churches can agree.

In some areas, this was Pace Egg Day, also known as Paste Egg

Day, when children went Pace Egging. They carried hard-boiled eggs with dyed shells and rolled them down the hillsides until the shells broke. Then they were eaten. This was sometimes called Egg Jawping, especially if one egg was used to break another. Pace Egg rolling ceremonies were held throughout the county; Pace Egg plays were also popular in the West Riding. The name pace or paste egg may come from Paaskaeg, deriving from paschal or pesach, the ancient reference to Easter and the Jewish passover. The egg is a symbol of new life and in some areas, these eggs were called Troll Eggs, the day being Troll Egg Day.

Since 1876, hymns have been sung from the north-west tower of Beverley Minster today. Also at Ilkley, the people would climb Beamsley Beacon to watch the sun rise and after noon today, lads in moorland villages would forcibly snatch the shoes off young girls and keep them until a ransom was paid for their return. This was known as Buckle Snatching Day.

Easter Sunday was the day for Yorkshire folk to wear new clothes, or at least a new item. Good luck was ensured by someone nipping the wearer while saying "Nip for new."

Easter Monday; Legging Day; Gawthorpe Coal Carrying Day —At Gawthorpe near Osset, local miners run an uphill course of almost one mile while carrying a sack of coal. The event was started in 1963. It is also known as a Legging Day in parts of Yorkshire because children attempted to trip one another with well aimed kicks to the ankles. In some areas, Easter eggs were rolled today, and so it was called Troll Egg Day, a name also given to Easter Sunday. Egg Jawping also occurred.

Low Sunday; Quasimodo Sunday — The Sunday after Easter, so-called because church ceremonial is more low-key than Easter Sunday. Catecumens, having worn white at their baptism, would dispense with it today. Quasimodo comes from the Latin introit of the day which begins, "Quasi modo geniti..."

Hock Monday and Hock Tuesday — The second Monday and Tuesday after Easter Sunday, the days following Low Sunday. Women could catch and bind any man they found and extract money from him. This was paid to the church. Likewise, men could demand money from women they caught. Hock Monday was for the men to do the chasing; Hock Tuesday was for the women. Parish tax collectors were also allowed to kiss any woman from whom they collected their dues!

APRIL

"April showers bring forth May flowers."

April's name may come from the Latin aprilis, which is derived from aperire, meaning 'to open'. It signifies the opening of buds and the beginning of life. In Anglo-Saxon times, it was called Easturmonath in honour of Eastre, goddess of the east and of the rising sun. Our very Christian festival of Easter is also named in her honour.

An all-embracing piece of wisdom is

"Never trust April sunshine."

Days in April

1 April — All Fools Day

Making fools of people is a national sport. In Scotland, today is Huntigowk Day or Hunt the Gowk Day, a gowk being a fool or a cuckoo. The term gowk was used at Whitby and Skipton while in some parts of Yorkshire, the fool was called an April noddy. In most areas, the jokes have to be perpetrated before noon otherwise they are ineffective. Two verses remind us of this:

"April noddy's past and gone
You're a fool and I am none."

The other, from Swaledale, was:

"April feul is past and gone,
An' thoo's a feul for thinking on."

There are many ways of making a fool; one was for the trickster to ask the victim to carry a letter to someone. When that person received it, he would say it was not for him, but for another person. And so the gowk would take it to the next person, who said it was for someone else ... and so ad infinitum. Other jokes included sending a youngster for a long stand, a bucket of steam or a pint of pigeon's milk — or any other stupid task. 1, 2 and 3 April are also known as blind days — days which are ill omened for the sowing of seeds.

5 April — Old Lady Day; Latter Lady Day

This has no association with old ladies, but is named from the calendar changes of 1752. The real Lady Day is 25 March. Cold weather is said to occur on this day.

"On Lady Day the latter,
Cawd cums alang t'watter!"

14 April — Cuckoo Day; St. Tiburtius' Day

Yorkshire folk believe cuckoos arrive for their summer visit and their distinctive call is heard around this time. There is an old verse:

"The cuckoo sings from St. Tiburtius' Day to St. John's Day."

Today is the feast day of St. Tiburtius, and St. John's Day is 24 June (Midsummer Day). There is an old Yorkshire saying which goes:

"When you hear the cuckoo shout, it's tahme ti plant your taties out."

19 April — Primrose Day

Benjamin Disraeli, the former Prime Minister died on 19 April 1881 and Queen Victoria sent a wreath of primroses for his grave.

They were not his favourite flower, but everyone thought they were and so Primrose Day was instituted. It is remembered in parts of the Dales.

23 April — Garter Day; St. George's Day; a Borrowing Day

The flag of St. George is flown in Yorkshire because George is our patron saint. Famous for fighting dragons, he has many Yorkshire emulators like those who fought the Nunnington Worm, the Sexhow Worm, the Handale Serpent, the Slingsby Serpent and the Dragon of Wantley. George is also patron saint of Germany, Venice, Aragon, Portugal, Ferrara, Greece, soldiers, armourers, chivalry, butchers, cavalrymen, saddlers, Boy Scouts and many churches. In spite of this, he was demoted by the Pope in 1969 because there is no proof he existed. He may be a myth. His feast day was abolished by the Vatican although he is mentioned in the Mass of the Day and remains England's patron saint.

Today is a Borrowing Day because a farmer can assess the value of his crops and use it as a bargaining point if he wants to borrow money. The lender of the money makes similar assessments.

The first Garter Day occurred on this date in 1344. Edward III was holding court when his lady friend, Joan, Countess of Kent and Salisbury, dropped her garter. She was deeply embarrassed by ribald comments and laughter, but the gallant King picked it up and bound it around his own knee, saying, *Honi soit qui mal y pense* which means, "Evil is to him who evil thinks". He said the garter would be honoured thereafter.

24 April — the Eve of St. Mark; Church Watching Eve; Chaff Riddling Night

In the North Riding, it was customary for some to visit the parish church and watch on the Eve of St. Mark. The watcher settled in the porch and it was believed that, at midnight, the spectral figures of those who were to die during the coming year would pass by. There are several accounts of watchers, including James Haw at Burniston near Bedale, seeing themselves — and later dying! Haw used to watch every year. It was important that a watcher never fell asleep on watch otherwise death was assured and when anyone commenced this ritual, it had to continue without a break until the end of one's life. Inevitably, the watcher saw himself or herself in spectral form.

A similar practice was chaff riddling, the venue being a barn. The watcher had to sit near the door and riddle chaff, and at midnight the spirits of all those who were to die in the coming year would pass by. An incident occurred at Malton when a woman watcher saw a coffin carried by two men — and she died within a year. Similar watching customs occurred at some crossroads in Yorkshire.

25 April — St. Mark's Day; ANZAC Day

This commemorates the landing of the ANZACS at Gallipoli in 1915 — ANZAC means Australian and New Zealand Army Corps.

27 April — St. Sitha's Day

Sitha! A Yorkshire saint — but she's not. She's Italian and her other name is Zita. She died, aged 12, in 1278.

30 April — Walpurgis Night; the Eve of May Day

Tonight, witches have a glorious feast on hill tops. It is also the day to insert sticks in the midden to protect crops against witchcraft and evil influences.

Miscellaneous Days in April

Grand National Day — Generally run on a Saturday in April (or sometimes March), the Grand National is the world's greatest steeplechase. Run over a course of four and a half miles (7.2km), the race started in 1839 at Aintree, near Liverpool and has featured many Yorkshire winners. It is also the day for Yorkshire gardeners to prune their roses or plant new rose bushes.

Tortoise Racing Day — Tortoise racing is popular in some districts. They carry toy jockeys and race around billiard tables.

Good Shepherd Sunday — At Glaisdale in the North York Moors in mid-April, sheep, shepherds and their dogs are blessed by the Vicar.

MAY

"Never cast a clout 'til May is out."

The old Dutch name for May was Bloumaand, month of blossom, which indicates its floral splendour. In Anglo-Saxon times, it was called Thri-milch, the lush growth enabling cows to be milked thrice daily.

The present name probably comes from the Roman festival of Maia. She was mother of the messenger god, Mercury, to whom sacrifices were offered on the first of this month. Another possibility is that May evolved from the Sanskrit *mah*, meaning growth, or the month's name might result from being dedicated by Romulus to the Roman senators known as *majores*.

It is considered unlucky to marry in May and among other Yorkshire lore are the following:

"On t' fost o' May, a good gull'll lay."

and

"Ye mon't wesh blankets i' May,
Or else you'll wesh your soul away."

With regard to never casting one's clothing until May is out, this probably refers not to the month, but to hawthorn blossom which is known as May. At Whitby, there was an old saying: "A wet May makes a long-tailed hay", suggesting a damp May was beneficial to hay. A windy May is even better and it is said that a snowstorm in May is worth a wagon load of hay.

Days in May

1 May — May Day; May Gosling Day; Birch Twig Day; Yellowhammer Day; Robin Hood's Day; Cattle Anointing Day; Dock Pudding Day

Maypoles and maypole dancing thrive in Yorkshire and fine examples of poles have been noted in Foston, Staithes, Roxby near Staithes, Slingsby near Malton, Langton near Malton, Masham,

42

Whitby, Coneysthorpe, Welburn, Clifton near York, Thorpe and Burnsall in Wharfedale, Sinnington, Skinningrove, Ovington near Richmond, Otley, Aldborough near Boroughbridge, Gawthorpe near Wakefield and the tallest of the lot at Barwick-in-Elmet near Leeds. There may be others.

Children in colourful clothes are taught the intricacies of maypole dancing which used to occur on May Day, sometimes with Morris Dancing as an added attraction. In recent years the dancing has been transferred to the Saturday or Sunday nearest May Day.

Maypole dancing was forbidden by the Puritans in 1644 because they regarded it as pagan but many villagers refused to destroy their maypoles. In 1701, Puritan Broadbrims, so called because of their hats, descended upon Sinnington near Pickering to halt the dancing. Others went to Helmsley, Kirkbymoorside and Slingsby, and at Slingsby there was "a great dordum of a fight", but the local lads managed to beat them off.

As a child, I remember this as May Gosling Day in Yorkshire's Eskdale when children played pranks upon one another before noon. These were like April Fool jokes, the victim being nicknamed "May Gosling".

The day is also known as Birch Twig Day because birch twigs were brought indoors to ward off evil, Yellowhammer Day because youths would chase and kill this bird, believing it drank the Devil's blood today, Robin Hood's Day because Robin Hood and Maid Marion featured as Lord and Lady of the May in the 16th century, and Cattle Anointing Day because farmers anointed their cattle to keep away evil spirits.

A cricket match, Black Hats versus White Hats, is held at Ilkley every May day and it is World Dock Pudding Championship Day at Hebden Bridge. Puddings are made from the young leaves of the sweet dock, with nettles, onions and oatmeal; they are fried with bacon and served with potatoes. The best are made in Calderdale. Some dock pudding contests are held on the fifth Sunday of Lent. (See March — Passion Sunday).

May Queens are elected in some villages, Robin Hood's Bay being one example. It is Hobby Horse Day in Cornwall, Cucumber Sowing Day in America when seeds are sown before sunrise by naked men, the eventual size of the cucumber being relative to the visible virility of the sower, and Lying Contest Day in Cumberland. Men compete for prizes for telling the biggest lie; this upset a Bishop of Carlisle who said he had never told a lie in his life — and was awarded first prize.

2 May — Rowan Tree Day; Rowan Tree Witch Day

In Yorkshire, houses, cattle and horses were decorated with sprigs of leaves from the rowan tree, otherwise known as mountain ash. In some areas, this was done on 3 May (Holy Rood Day). Since ancient times, this tree has been used to ward off witches and evil spirits.

To keep witches out of milking parlours, churn parts were made from rowan wood as were the handles of tools and horse whips. In some areas, the tree was known as witchwood or witch hazel.

7 May — St. John of Beverley's Day

John was born in AD 640 at Harpham between Bridlington and Driffield. He entered Whitby Abbey as a pupil of St. Hilda and in AD 687 became Bishop of Hexham. He ordained the renowned Venerable Bede. John retired to Beverley and died there, the Minster being successor to his early church. St. John was revered throughout England, and at Harpham, St. John's Well survives; it is said the water will cure sick cattle and his name is carved upon the stonework. The well is sometimes called The Drumming Well. (See my *Folk Tales from York and the Wolds*, written as Peter N. Walker). St. John is also honoured on 25 October.

11 to 14 May — Ice Saints' Days; Frost Saints' Days; Leaving Day

It is said there is always frost during Ice Saints' Day but I know of no test of its accuracy! The Ice or Frost Saints are: St. Mamertus (11 May), St. Pancras (12 May), St. Servatius (13 May) and St. Boniface (14 May). It is due to the likelihood of this chilly weather that Yorkshire shepherds say: "He who shears his sheep before St. Servatius's Day loves the wool more than the sheep" although May 13 is said to be beneficial for bean planting.

St. Pancras is not the patron saint of railway stations — the London station of that name was built on the site of a former St. Pancras Church. His feast day was a Leaving Day in Yorkshire, when workers left to find other employment.

15 May — Buttercup Day

A folk story says that a fair maid was terrorised by a huge serpent.

A gallant knight came by and, after a terrible fight, slew the monster. He was fatally wounded and as he lay dying, he plucked a buttercup and quoth to the maid; "Think of me when you first see a buttercup." No-one knows where this occurred, but see 23 April for some battles with Yorkshire serpents.

19 May — St. Dunstan's Day

In Yorkshire, no luck will follow a declaration of love made today.

25 May — St. Urban's Day

A well known saying tells us: "St. Urban brings summer."

29 May — Oak Apple Day; Chalky Back Day; Restoration Day; Nettle Day; Garland Day

Within living memory, there were nationwide celebrations today. Sprigs of oak were worn and there were special church services to commemorate the Restoration of the Monarchy. This happened when Charles II entered London after England had been a republic under Oliver Cromwell. 29 May was also the birthday of Charles II and the celebrations remind us that Charles concealed himself in an oak tree at Biscobel in Shropshire after his defeat at Worcester. That tree became known as the Royal Oak, a name given to many English inns.

In Yorkshire, there were special celebrations. Children expected a day off school, locking their teacher inside as they sang:

"Royal Oak Day, Twenty ninth o' May,
If thoo dissn't gi' us a holiday, we'll all run away."

In many villages, boys collected nettles and chased children who had forgotten to wear oak leaves; the culprits would be stung on their bare legs. Thus the day was known as Nettle Day. This happened in Boroughbridge, Richmond, Northallerton and the North York Moors but the practice appears to have dwindled after World War II. In some moorland villages, those who forgot to wear sprigs of oak were smothered in powdered chalk, hence Chalky Back Day.

In Derbyshire this is Garland Day when a picturesque garland on a huge, bell-shaped frame is carried through Castleton. It halts at inns where dances are performed and the procession ends at the church. In earlier times, garlands of May flowers were carried on May Day.

Miscellaneous Days in May

Spa Sunday, Spaw Sunday — Spaw is the old word for spa. On this first Sunday of the month, people would sip spa waters from a well near Hebden Bridge. The well was decorated and Morris dancers would entertain. An attempt to revive the custom in 1988 was unsuccessful.

Rogation Sunday; Rammalation Day; Gang Days — This is the Sunday before Ascension Day and the Rogation Days are the following Monday, Tuesday and Wednesday. Thursday is Ascension Day, the fortieth day after Easter.

In Yorkshire, Rogation Sunday was called Rammalation Day, but the four days together were called Rogationtide or Gang Days. Gang is a derivation of the dialect for go; parishioners would 'gang aroond" the parish boundaries to Beat the Bounds. Children would be lifted by the hands and feet and their bottoms bumped on the ground at the extremities of the parish.

Alternatively, the ground itself, or trees or rocks, would be thrashed with sticks at these points. This performance ensured the children never forgot the boundaries of their parish and they would similarly instruct the next generation.

Today, Beating the Bounds has been revived in some areas, Ripon, Swainby, Fylingdales, Bielby near Pocklington and Keighley being examples. At Richmond in Swaledale, the Riding and Perambulation of the Boundaries has been conducted every seven years since 1576. The procession is led by the Mayor with his bellman and cryer. Because one of the boundaries lies in the middle of the River Swale, wading boots are necessary; the Water Wader used to carry the Mayor into the water to inspect a boundary stone.

Near Kirkbymoorside, the Manor of Spaunton's boundary inspection entails a 30-mile hike spread over two days, and in bygone times, the processions would halt beneath an oak tree where the priest would say Mass and preach a sermon. These became known as Gospel Oaks.

Beating the Bounds can occur on any of the Rogation Days and upon Ascension Day.

The Eve of the Ascension — Although it is a moveable date, the Eve of the Ascension always falls on a Wednesday — Rogation Wednesday in fact — and it witnesses a curious custom at Whitby. The ancient ceremony of the Planting of the Penny Hedge, otherwise known as the Horngarth Ceremony, has been conducted for about 825 years. It is continued by a small party which gathers at 9 am on the mud of the upper harbour. Suitably dressed, one member holds a horn while two others carry bundles of small pliable branches and twigs. Some sticks are planted upright and others are woven between them to create a short, flimsy fence. When this is complete, the horn is sounded and the blower calls "Out on ye, out on ye, out on ye". The words *"for this heinous crime"* used to follow, but have been discontinued. The knife which cuts the stakes should cost no more than one penny, and the finished hedge must withstand at least three tides. The building of this fence is a family penance for the murder of a monk/hermit in 1159 and this fragile barrier has withstood all tides for more than 820 years until 27 May 1981 when a freak tide covered it. this brought the penance to an end — nonetheless, the custom continues for the sake of Yorkshire tradition, the penance having been completed. Another freak tide covered it in 1991. A detailed account is in my *Murders and Mysteries of the North York Moors* as by Peter N. Walker, (Hale).

Ascension Day — The day Christ ascended into heaven. Yorkshire country folk would collect rain water on this day, believing it contained properties which would cure ailments. The Anglican Church calls it Holy Thursday but Catholics use that name for Maundy Thursday.

Whit Sunday; Walking Day — The seventh Sunday after Easter used to be the time for baptising children.They wore white garments, and so this became White Sunday, later Whit Sunday. Churches and chapels held open air services.

One old custom was for churches to sell ale; it was known as Church Ale or Whitsun Ale and the income was to defray church expenses. Church Ale was sold at other times being variously known as Bride Ale, Lamb Ale, Midsummer Ale, etc.

The Bellerby Feast was held on Whit Sunday and was recently revived at Bellerby in Wensleydale. It included a sword dance. In some towns, processions led by brass bands paraded to raise cash for charity; they referred to this as a Walking Day. The old Calderdale Whit Walk and Sing was revived in 1990, ending with a picnic at the Piece Hall, Halifax.

Whitsuntide is the week following this Sunday, the time for Yorkshiremen to buy their new suits. Yorkshire lads would also be given new suits at this time.

Whit Monday — A walking contest, the Bradford Whit Walk is held. Covering thirty miles, the winner receives the Hammond Cup named after the man who founded the race in 1903. This is also the day of the Richmond Meet, originally a gathering of cyclists; it has now developed into a larger assembly with sporting contests and entertainments and has been moved to the Spring Bank Holiday, the last Monday in May.

Cyclists' Sunday — On the second Sunday of May, a service for cyclists is held at St. Michael's Church, Coxwold near Thirsk. Cycles and cyclists ancient and modern attend and the event began in 1926. Cyclists call it Coxwold Sunday.

JUNE

"A swarm of bees in June is worth a silver spoon."

The Anglo-Saxon name for Seremonath, the dry month and the time of haysel; the old Dutch was Zomer-maand, the summer month while yet another name was Lida serra, joy time. The consulate of Junius Brutus might be a source of the name, the term *junius* indicating young; alternatively, the goddess Juno, queen of heaven, might be honoured. It was the fourth month in the Roman calendar; Numa placed it No. 6 around BC 700 where it has remained.

Although June is sometimes called Flaming June because of the sun's heat, the Yorkshire farmer welcomes rain. There is a saying that "A dripping June puts all in tune" while another says, "June damp and warm does the farmer no harm".

Days in June

2 June — Coronation Day

In 1953, Her Majesty Queen Elizabeth II was crowned at Westminster Abbey.

8 June — St. Medard's Day; St. William of York's Day

Little-known St. Medard is the patron of brewers, peasants and prisoners; he is invoked for fruitfulness in child-bearing and of crops and harvest. In Yorkshire, when it rained, farmers said, 'It's St. Medard watering his colts". Another verse went:

"Should St. Medard's Day be wet,
It will rain for forty yet;
At least until St. Barnabas
The summer sun won't favour us."

St. William, a miracle worker at York, was a mild, likeable fellow who was appointed Archbishop of York by Pope Anastasius IV, but William was probably murdered by poison in 1154. His many miracles are commemorated in stained glass in York Minster.

10 June — White Rose Day

This is a Scottish festival, unconnected with Yorkshire Day (see 1 August).

11 June — Barnaby Day; St. Barnabas' Day

In some parts of Yorkshire this was called Barnaby Bright. St. Barnabas was a former labourer who travelled with St. Paul and is thought to have been related to St. Mark. He worked in Rome before going to Milan where he became the town's first bishop. Before the calendar changes in 1752, Barnaby Day was the longest day of the year, the traditional time to begin the hay harvest. Barnaby Fairs were held, at which Barnaby Tarts were eaten and the day was one of celebration. Boroughbridge held its Barnaby Fair on the Tuesday nearest 22 June, the old feast of St. Barnabas; the street known as the Horsefair is named after it.

An old saying, now inaccurate, says,

"Barnaby Bright, Barnaby bright,
The longest day and shortest night."

Another is "At Barnabas, put the scythe to the grass."

21 June — The Longest Day

The first day of summer. At Stonehenge, Companions of the Most Ancient Order of Druids keep a midnight vigil before sunrise over the ancient stone circle. In Yorkshire, there is a similar stone circle near Ilton, close to Masham. This is a folly built around 1820 to create work for the staff of Swinton Park estate.

22 June — St. Alban's Day; Weeding Day

There is an old belief that weeds cut down today will not re-appear, provided they have been cut either at full moon or during the afternoon. St. Alban, a Roman soldier, was Britain's first martyr, beheaded in AD 303 or 304 for his faith at the place now called St. Albans.

23 June — Midsummer's Eve; St. John's Eve; Need Fire Night; Mugwort Digging Night

Various charms were practised to discover the name of one's future spouse. Yorkshire youths gathered spores from ferns hoping their magic would attract the girl of their dreams. Rural folks would dig beneath the mugwort looking for magic coal to protect them against lightning, plague and burning. St. John's Wort was collected and hung near the doors and windows of Yorkshire farm houses as a protection against evil. Young girls collected hempseed and scattered it in the belief it would reveal the name of their true love. The day was also known as Need Fire Night; when fire was a precious commodity, flames were carried by runners to every house in the village; the occupants lit their fires and ensured they continued to burn.

24 June — Midsummer Day; St. John the Baptist's Day

A quarter day when Yorkshire tenants paid their rents; a beetle racing day in the Vale of Evesham (cockroaches not allowed) and a well-dressing day in Derbyshire. For Yorkshire horticulturalists, it was the day to cut thistles:

"Cut your thistles before St. John,
And you'll have two instead of one!"

There is another verse about thistles which says:

"Cut thistles in May, they grow in a day;
Cut thistles in June, that is too soon,
Cut thistles in July, and then they will die."

The St. John whose day we celebrate was St. John the Baptist; when Herod gave a feast, Salome pleased him so much that the King said she may have whatever she wished. She wanted the head of John the Baptist on a plate at table, and so Herod ordered the saint's execution. This was two years before Christ was crucified.

29 June — Saints Peter and Paul Day

A curious saying for bakers states that if it rains on St. Peter's Day, the bakers will have to carry double flour and single water. If it is dry, they will have to carry single flour and double water. One old saying adds that if it rains on apple trees today, then the saints are watering the orchards. If not, the crop will be poor.

St. Peter, the first Pope, was crucified in AD 64 by the Emperor Nero. St. Paul was martyred in Rome on the same day. He was beheaded and it is said his head bounced three times on the ground — at each place, a fountain appeared.

Miscellaneous Days in June

Alexandra Rose Day — Rose emblems are sold to raise money for the hospital fund inaugurated by Queen Alexandra in 1912.

Derby Day — The first Wednesday in June when Yorkshire horse owners, trainers and punters hope for a winner.

Trinity Sunday — The Sunday after Whit Sunday. On the bridge at Kirkham Priory near Malton, a bird fair was held from 2 am until sunrise. Birds were exchanged, boy met girl and much feasting was enjoyed.

Corpus Christi — A church festival held on the Thursday after Trinity Sunday, now called 'The Body and Blood of Christ'. Instituted by Pope Urban IV in 1264, the day is celebrated with performances of religious dramas by trade guilds. All celebrations were banned at the Reformation, but York, Coventry, Chester and Middlesbrough have been centres of these revived plays or processions.

Greyhound Derby Day — The fourth Saturday in June; held at the White City stadium in London, when Yorkshire folk go to the dogs.

Drinking Day — The first National Drinking Day was 20 June 1989, aimed at the sensible drinking of alcohol. At lot of Yorkshire remain unaware of this day, and my suggestion is that it be combined with Father's Day.

Halifax Thump Sunday — The Sunday following 24th June which marks the beginning of a traditional fair known as Halifax Thump.

Hepworth Feast Day — Celebrated on the last Monday in June since 1665, this marks the deliverance of Hepworth, near Holmfirth, from a plague. The festivities include a procession and hymn singing.

Walkington Hay Ride Day — On the third Sunday of June there is a procession of historic horse drawn vehicles between Walkington and Beverley. Replicating a journey made by hay carts, it was revived in 1967 to raise money for charity.

JULY

"In Yorkshire, winter ends in July and starts again in August."

Because meadows flowered and cattle were turned into them during July, the Anglo-Saxons named it maedmonath. Its present name came from Mark Anthony who called it July in honour of Julius Caesar; it was previously called Quinctillis, the fifth month where it remained until January and February were added.

Few Yorkshire sayings are linked to the weather this month but one says that the first Friday of July is always wet. Another goes: "Nivver trust a July sky," while yet another suggests that "Much thunder in July injures wheat and barley."

Days in July

2 July — St. Mary's Day

A Yorkshire saying goes: "If it rains on St. Mary, it'll rain for fower weeks." There are many saints called Mary and the origin of this feast is obscure; the principal one is 15 August while that of Mary Magdalen is 22 July. Lady Day is 25 March and I'm not sure which of the other Marys is honoured today. On this day in 1644, the Battle of Marston Moor was fought near York.

3 July onwards to 11 August — the Dog Days

The Romans named these the Dog Days because they believed that Sirius, the dog star, rose and set with the sun to provide additional heat. Thus the Dog Days are a long, hot period of summer. It has long been thought that Sirius affects dogs; no-one knows its effects upon Yorkshire terriers and Airedales.

4 July — Bullions Day; Old Midsummer Eve; Independence Day in the USA

Throughout the north of England and Scotland, it is said that "If the deer rise dry and lie down dry on Bullions Day, there will be a good harvest." The name Bullions comes from the French St Martin

Bouillant. Under his alias of St. Martin of Tours, the saint has another feast day on 11 November.

This was Midsummer Eve until the calendar changes of 1752 and throughout the north of England, bonfires were lit in celebration.

6 July — Cucumber Day

Until the calendar changes of 1752, this was the day when discerning Yorkshire gardeners planted cucumbers.

"Plant cucumber seeds on sixth July,
You'll have cucumbers, wet or dry."

7 July — St. Hedda's Day

Few churches are named after Hedda but one is at Egton Bridge in the Esk Valley. "The village missed by the Reformation" boasts a magnificent Catholic church more fitted to a city than a tiny moorland village. St. Hedda, who died in AD 705, was a contemporary of the Venerable Bede and one-time bishop of Winchester.

9 July — The Feast Day of Saints John Fisher and Thomas More

Cardinal John Fisher was executed by Henry VIII because he refused to accept Henry as head of the church in England. Born at Beverley in 1469, John Fisher was parish priest at Lythe near Whitby, later becoming Bishop of Rochester. He is known as St. John of Rochester, being canonised by the Pope in 1935.

Thomas More also suffered a martyr's death; he was beheaded nine days after John Fisher for his stance against Henry VIII's attempted destruction of the Catholic church in England. More's most famous book is *Utopia*.

11 July — St. Benedict's Day; Thorn Bawming Day

A time to decorate hawthorn trees with garlands of flowers. For the sowing of peas associated with this day, see 21 March. St. Benedict (AD 480-547) founded the Benedictine Order of monks; Benedictines built many abbeys in Yorkshire, the most modern of which is at Ampleforth.

15 July — St. Swithin's Day

One of the best known weather prognosticating days with this saying:

"St. Swithin's Day, if thou dost rain,
For forty days it will remain;
St. Swithin's Day, if thou be fair,
For forty day t'will rain neea mair."

There are other beliefs, such as "Till St. Swithin's day be past, apples are not fit to taste", and "All the tears that St. Swithin can cry, St. Bartholomew's dusty month wipes dry." St. Bartholomew's Day is 24 August.

St. Swithin was Bishop of Winchester in AD 852 and said he did not wish to be buried inside the church. A century after his death, an attempt was made to transfer his remains into the building, but a downpour made the work impossible. It was interpreted as the saint's wish to lie undisturbed. The rainy legend of St. Swithin thus began. When it rains on St. Swithin's Day, it is said he is christening the apples.

A proclamation announcing Seamer Fair, near Scarborough, established by Richard II, is read on St. Swithin's Day, even though the fair lapsed in the 1930s. The Lord and Lady of the Manor read the proclamation under an oak tree on the village green and scatter coins for the children.

20 July — St. Margaret's Day

Yorkshire gardeners would ensure their turnips were planted on St. Margaret's Day and it is a good day for picking pears.

"If St. Margaret's brings the first pear,
Pears will be plentiful during the year."

There is a more ominous belief that floods occur on or near her feast day. Certainly, cloud bursts are not uncommon in July, and they are often known as St. Margaret's floods. In July, 1892, a devasting flood occurred in Langtoft in the Yorkshire Wolds.

22 July — St. Mary Magdalen's Day

Maidens on the North York Moors would attempt to identify their future husband by mixing a potion of rum, gin and red wine with treacle, honey and sugar. Various rituals followed before the concoction was drunk — and it was believed the drinkers would dream of their beloved. It was said that if it rains on St. Mary Magdalen, she is washing her handkerchief before visiting her cousin, St. James the Great. His feast day is 25 July; see also 2 July.

25 July — Feast of St. James the Greater; St. Christopher's Day; Turnip Planting Day; Chicory Cutting Day

St. James was the first apostle to die for Christ and St. Christopher is the patron saint of travellers. Known to country folk as Turnip Planting Day, Chicory Cutting Day and, on the coast, the day that oysters come into season, children made small grottos of oyster shells. It was said, "He who eats oysters on St. James' Day will not want during the coming year", and chicory was thought to make anyone who wore it become invisible.

Miscellaneous Days in July

Gormire Day — The last Saturday of term at Ampleforth College. The boys had to travel from Ampleforth College to Lake Gormire below Sutton Bank by any means except motor vehicles. Upon arrival, they had a picnic. Most of them walked or rode bicycles but one year, four boys hired a camel from a local zoo. The camel survived but the outing has been discontinued.

Rush Bearing Days — These were widespread in country areas, particularly in the north of England in July or August. They were recently revived at Haworth and Sowerby Bridge in Yorkshire, these ceremonies being in September (see September). Grasmere selects the Saturday nearest the feast of St. Anne (26 July). The celebrations vary widely but stem from the days when church floors were covered with rushes which had to be replaced; processions of youngsters carried out the old stock and brought in the new amid much ceremonial and feasting.

Kilburn Feast Day — Beginning on the Sunday after 7 July, the village of Kilburn near Coxwold holds its annual four-day feast. There is a mock Mayor and Mayoress, along with feasting, games and a race to the famous White Horse. (See 9 November).

Oxenhope Straw Race Day — A day in July when teams of runners race from pub to pub around Oxenhope near Keighley while carrying bales of straw.

Well Dressing Day — Dore, near Sheffield, was in Derbyshire until 1974 but is now in South Yorkshire. It hosts a well dressing day on the second Saturday of July.

56

Blessing the Boats — On a Sunday in July, the boats of Whitby's fishing fleet are blessed at a harbourside service. The date depends upon the high tide and can vary by as much as three weeks.

Mapplewell and Staincross Sing — On the third Sunday of July, a mass sing-song and fair take place at Staincross near Barnsley. Money is raised for a hospital charity.

AUGUST

"Dry August and warm does harvest no harm."

Known to the Romans as Sextilis, August was the sixth month before January and February were added. The Emperor, Augustus, regarded it as his lucky month and in BC 8, named it in his honour. The Anxlo-Saxon name was Weodmonath, the month of weeds, but this term weed meant vegetation in general.

In Yorkshire, it was said "A rainy August makes a hard bread crust!" while rural wisdom said, "Seea monny a fog i' August, seea monny mists i' winter." This is reinforced by a belief that August's weather will be mirrored the following February — a dry August means a dry February and a wet August means a wet February although an unusually warm first week in August threatens a long, white winter.

Days in August

1 August — Yorkshire Day; White Rose Day; Lammas Day; Bilberry Day; Minden Day; the Gule of August

Founded in 1975 by the Yorkshire Ridings Society, Yorkshire Day is very important for Yorkshire folk. It is celebrated by wearing white roses, eating Yorkshire puddings and uttering greetings like "Now then" or "Ow ist tha?" with other choice phrases such as "Eee baa gum." The purpose is to remind everyone, including Yorkshire people, that the three famous Ridings were not abolished in the 1974 boundary changes.

Those changes did create the new administrative counties of North Yorkshire, West Yorkshire, South Yorkshire, Cleveland and Humberside, but did not abolish the North Riding, the East Riding and the West Ridings of Yorkshire which have existed for more that 1111 years. A declaration to that effect is ceremoniously read at the Bars of the City of York on Yorkshire Day and hotels, inns and restaurants offer Yorkshire fare. White roses are on sale, either natural or in silk, and other fund raising events, such as the making of giant Yorkshire puddings are organised for the benefit of Yorkshire charities.

This is also Minden Day. The Battle of Minden was fought on 1 August 1759 during the Seven Years' War and members of a Yorkshire Regiment took part. Troops picked white roses before the battle to wear in their caps. At the non-Yorkshire side of the Pennines, officers of the Lancashire Fusiliers eat a rose on Minden Day. They are not considered true Fusiliers until they have eaten a rose. It is not wise for Yorkshire folk to enquire about the colour of those roses.

This is also Lammas Day when fairs and festivals were held throughout Yorkshire. One Lammastide Fair was revived by the Yorkshire Countrywomen's Association at Thornton-le-dale in 1985. Lammas, otherwise known as the Gule of August, was a great pagan festival which celebrated the first fruits of the harvest. Later, the church used the occasion to celebrate a Loaf Mass, with loaves made from the first ripened corn. Loaves were blessed at Mass, and the communion wafers were made from that first ripened corn. Known as Lowermass in Cumbria, it is believed the term Lammas is a derivation of Loaf Mass.

The Irish celebrate the Sunday nearest today as Bilberry Day or Bilberry Sunday when open air jollifications mark the picking of the ripe bilberries; the day is variously known as Blaeberry Sunday, Whortleberry Sunday, Hurt Sunday, Heathberry Sunday or, in Ireland, Fraughan Sunday. The Irish name for this day is Domhnach na bh Fraochog or bhFraochan Sunday. In Scotland, today was a quarter day when rents were due, at one time being paid partly in ripe corn and the name Gule probably comes from the Welsh *gwyl* meaning festival.

One old custom was that certain areas of land used for crops were thrown open for common use this day. The land could then be used for pasture or other purposes, and often remained available until the following spring.

There is a saying that the corn ripens as much by night as it does by day after Lammas; that warmth reminds us that it is also one of the continuing Dog Days.

9 August — St. Oswald's Day; Rush Bearing Day

Few villages are named after the patron of their church; one is Oswaldkirk near Helmsley, the name meaning Oswald's church.

Yorkshire boasts several churches with Oswald as patron. Oswald was King of Northumbria and a friend of St. Aiden. A kindly man, Oswald once gave three beggars a silver dish containing his dinner. Another St. Oswald became Archbishop of York in AD 972 and his feast day is 28 February; he is St. Oswald of Worcester.

Many rush bearing ceremonies occur on or around this St. Oswald's Day. In Yorkshire, they have been revived at Haworth and Sowerby Bridge, albeit on the first Sunday of September. (see also July). Hay is sometimes strewn as an alternative.

10 August — St. Lawrence's Day; Lazy Lawrence Day

There is a curious saying which goes:

"Lazy Lawrence let me go,
Don't hold me summer and winter too."

The name 'Lazy Lawrence' comes from St. Lawrence of Rome, martyred in AD 258 by being slowly roasted on a gridiron. He asked his captors to be turned, saying "This side is quite done". His torturers interpreted that as a surpreme example of laziness. The Benedictine Abbey of Ampleforth is dedicated to St. Lawrence.

12 August — The Glorious Twelfth; Bowlingtide

The Glorious Twelfth of August is the beginning of the grouse shooting season, unless it falls on a Sunday. Grouse need to be culled to ensure healthy stocks, and the income from shooting parties maintains the heather and the moors. The season ends on 10 December.

At Bradford, this was Bowlingtide; beginning today, Bowlingtide Week was a holiday for the millworkers, and fairs were held.

18 August — St. Helena's (Helen's) Day

At Walton near Wetherby, water from St. Helen's Well was said to cure ailments, especially eye diseases, if rubbed on with a rag. Helena, also known as Helen, was the mother of the Roman emperor, Constantine the Great. The famous highwayman, Swift Nick Nevison, fell asleep near St. Helen's Well and was almost captured — but he fooled local men into letting him go. Their daftness earned them the name of Walton Calves.

20 August — St. Oswin's Day

Oswin was cousin to St. Oswald (9 August). Upon Oswald's death,

60

he ruled the Kingdom of Deira which was part of Northumbria; Deira included the North York Moors. Handsome, courteous and humble, Oswin was a friend of St. Aiden who said, "This king will not live long — I never saw so humble a prince and this people is not worthy to have such a ruler."

Aiden was right. Another cousin, Oswy, wanted to rule the whole of Northumbria and a henchman killed Oswin at Gilling near Richmond in AD 651. Oswy became King of Northumbria which covered an area from the Scottish border to the northern banks of the Humber — hence North Humber Land. Oswy's cousin, Hilda, became Abbess of Whitby (see 17 November).

24 August — Bartlemy Day; St. Bartholomew's Day

On this day, many villages and towns held gigantic Bartholomew Fairs or Bartle Fairs. One was at Smithfield in London; this ran from 1133 until 1752 when the calendar was changed. The fair was transferred to 13 September, but has not been held since 1855.

At West Ardsley near Wakefield, the Former Lee Gap horse fair is held. This is said to be England's oldest horse fair, established in 1100 by a charter granted by Henry I to Nostel Priory. (See 17 September for the Latter Lee Gap horse fair).

West Witton in Wensleydale, whose church is dedicated to St. Bartholomew, has long held a St. Bartholomew's Day fair, more recently known as Witton Feast. A fascinating custom survives.

It is Burning Old Bartle and occurs on the Saturday nearest St. Bartholomew's Day. This brings Witton Feast to an end. An effigy of Old Bartle is carried in procession to the outskirts where it is ceremoniously burnt. As the procession moves around the village, it halts at several places to chant the following rhyme:

> "In Penhill Crags he tore his rags,
> At Hunter's Thorn he blew his horn,
> At Capplebeck Stee he brake his knee,
> At Grisgill Beck he brake his neck,
> At Wadham's End he couldn't fend,
> At Grisdale End he met his end."

Each time the verse is chanted, a caller shouts "Shout, lads, shout" and all the assembled people call "Hip, hip, hooray."

West Witton lies below the mysterious Penhill, rich in lore, legend and mystery. One of the great stories of Yorkshire concerns the

Giant of Penhill but the Burning of Old Bartle is thought to have its origins in a ritual involving St. Bartholomew or possibly an ancient sun deity known as Baal.

Another theory is that Bartle was a horse thief who is still punished by the villagers and yet a further suggestion is that the ceremony stems from pagan times when the last sheaf of corn was supposed to contain the corn spirit. The last sheaf was burnt to destroy the evil of that spirit. There is a more complete account, plus the story of the Giant of Penhill, in my *Folk Stories from the Yorkshire Dales* written as Peter N. Walker (Hale).

Autumn is said to begin on St. Bartholomew's Day. An old Yorkshire saying goes: "St. Bartholomew brings the dew" and others tell us "As is St. Bartholomew's Day, so is the entire autumn." The forty days rain which might have begun on St. Swithin's Day, is supposed to end on St. Bartholomew's Day —"All the tears that St. Swithin can cry, St. Bartlemy's mantle can wipe dry" — and shepherds said that if this day began with a mist and a hoar frost, cold weather would follow and a hard winter lay ahead.

29 August — St. John's Wort Day

St. John's Wort was supposed to flower around Midsummer's Day when red spots appeared on its leaves. They were believed to commemorate the beheading of St. John the Baptist. There are several varieties of the wort and in bygone times, Yorkshire folk thought that if the flower was in a window, it would protect the house against ghosts, witches, evil spirits and thunderbolts (see 23 June).

Miscellaneous Days in August

Semerwater Day — Since 1956, on the first Sunday of August, a church service has been held on the shores of Lake Semerwater in the Yorkshire Dales. It commemorates Christ's teaching from a boat.

Egton Bridge Old Gooseberry Show Day — One of the few surviving shows dedicated to gooseberries, this takes place on the second Tuesday of August at Egton Bridge near Whitby. The Egton Bridge Old Gooseberry Society was established in 1800; the prizes are for the heaviest berries in various categories. The show is open to the public during the afternoons.

Rose Queen Day — On the first Tuesday of August at Littlebeck near Whitby, a Rose Queen is crowned and, with her attendants, floats downstream on a raft.

Ebor Day — The Ebor Handicap is York's premier horse race, being run on York Racecourse at the Knavesmire on the Wednesday of York's renowned three-day meeting in mid-August. First run in 1844, the Ebor is a classic race; the same meeting hosts the Yorkshire Oaks and Gimcrack Stakes.

Burnsall Feast Day — In honour of St. Wilfred, this has been held in August since medieval times at Burnsall in Wharfedale. It includes the famous Fell Race during which runners climb to 1300 feet on Burnsall Fell (see 12 October).

St. Wilfred's Feast Day — On the Saturday before the first Monday in August, Wilfred pies are eaten in Ripon and a man dressed as St. Wilfred rides a horse through the City. Accompanied by civic dignitaries, he is followed by colourful floats to the Cathedral where a service is held. This should not be confused with St. Wilfred's official feast day which is 12 October. See also Easter Sunday (March). The Blowing of the Wakeman's Horn, a custom practised since Anglo-Saxon times, continues in Ripon which is the smallest city in Yorkshire, and may be the smallest in Britain.

SEPTEMBER

"September dries up wells and breaks down bridges."

Known originally as Gerstmonath, barley month, the Anglo-Saxons also called it Haefestmonath, harvest month. The name September comes from the Roman seventh month — Septem — introduced by Romulus in BC 753. The addition of January and February made September our ninth month. Being the month of harvests, it incorporates a good deal of folk lore and there are some curious verses to celebrate the bringing-home of the last sheaf of corn, the mell sheaf. One goes:

"We hev her, we hev her,
A coo is a tether
At oor toon end.
A yowe an' a lamb,
A pot an' a pan.
May wa git seeafe in,
Wiv oor harvest-yam,
Wiv a sup o' good yal
An' sum hawpence ti spend."

Another verse from Wensleydale is this:

"John Metcalfe has gitten all shorn an' mawn,
All but a few standards an' a bit o' lowse corn.
We hev her, we hev her, fast in a tether,
Cum help us ti hod her! Hurrah, hurrah, hurrah."

There is a widespread belief that thunder in September indicates a good crop of grain and fruit for the coming year, but perhaps the best known of weather sayings is:

"September blow soft till the fruit's in the loft."

Days in September

1 September — St. Giles Day

In the past, many towns and villages celebrated St. Giles Day with fairs but this custom has disappeared. Nowadays, a reminder comes in "Fair on St. Giles Day, fair for the whole month". But this word "fair" indicates the state of the weather!

3 September — Denby Dale Pie Day

In 1988, a giant bicentenary pie was baked and shared between 50,000 people. The first giant pie was baked here in 1788 to celebrate the return to sanity of King George III, and periodically, massive pies have been baked to celebrate major events. A huge pie dish serves as a flower bed outside Denby Dale's Pie Hall.

14 September — Holy Rood Day; Rood Mass Day; Nutting Day

Holy Rood is another name for the Holy Cross. Today is the Feast of the Exaltation of the Holy Cross, known to the Anglo-Saxons as Rood Mass Day. The celebration began in the third century when Emperor Constantine of Rome saw a blazing cross in the noon sky.

In Yorkshire, there is an old saying:

"If dry be the buck's horn
On Holy Rood morn,
'Tis worth a kiss of gold.
But if wet it be seen,
'Ere Holy Rood e'en,
Bad harvest is foretold."

The subsequent English celebrations included a holiday for schoolchildren so they could gather nuts, so it became Nutting Day. It is said the Devil goes a-nutting on Nutting Day. On this day in 1752, there were riots against the changes to the old calendar.

15 September — Battle of Britain Day

Between August and October, 1940, as part of World War II, the German Luftwaffe waged a prolonged aerial attack on the south-east of England, but were beaten by the pilots and aircraft of the RAF. Winston Churchill termed this "The Battle of Britain". There is a curious belief that the weather on this day is fine for six years out of every seven.

17 September — Lee Gap Day

The Latter Lee Gap Horse Fair is held at West Ardsley near

Wakefield. (See 24 August for the Former Lee Gap Horse Fair.)

19 September — First Fruits Day

At Richmond, Yorkshire, on the Saturday nearest this day, the mayor presents two bottles of wine to the first farmer to take a sample of the new season's wheat to the market cross. One bottle is used to drink the mayor's health, the other is for the farmer himself. Richmond's corn market used to be the largest in England.

21 September — St. Matthew's Day; the autumn equinox

Autumn is thought to begin and a popular Yorkshire saying that "St. Matthew shuts up the bees and brings the cold, the rain and the dew." It was the day for buying new candles although a south wind indicates the remaining autumn will be mild. It is also the autumn equinox.

24 September — St. Robert of Knaresborough's Day

A twelfth century cave-dwelling saint, Robert lived at Knaresborough and his hermitage, known as St. Robert's Chapel, can still be seen in the cliffs above the River Nidd.

25 September — Stamford Bridge Pie Day

To commemorate the Battle of Stamford Bridge in 1066, a huge pie, and later lots of smaller pies, called Spear Pies, were baked in the shape of a boat and fitted with a skewer to represent a spear. An English soldier rowed beneath the bridge and thrust a spear upwards to kill a massive Viking who was holding the bridge. The pie-baking custom died out but was revived in 1966.

28 September — The Eve of Michaelmas; Nut Crack Eve

In rural churches, there was a quaint custom of cracking nuts this evening. I cannot find a reason, my only reference being "it was a night of great rejoicing and mysterious rites and ceremonies." The date of Nut Crack Eve or Nut Crack Night is in dispute, however, and some authorities believe it was on 29 September or 31 October. In Wensleydale, the Bainbridge Horn is sounded every evening from today until Shrove Tuesday.

29 September — Michaelmas Day; Hipping Day; Nut Crack Night; Porch Watching Day; Goose Day; Hiring Day

This is the feast of St. Michael the Archangel who was a spirit and not a human being. Mass was said in churches throughout the world but in Yorkshire, it is the day the devil puts his foot on brambles! In other words, brambles are not very nice to eat after today. It is a Nut Cracking Day in Surrey (see 28 September), a Church Porch Watching Day in some areas (see 24 April) and a Goose Day in the countryside. It is said that Queen Elizabeth I was eating goose this day when she received news of the defeat of the Spanish Armada. Since then, it has been customary to eat goose on Michaelmas Day. Public thanksgiving for this victory was offered on 20 August 1588.

The Lord Mayor of London is elected today, it was National Police Day in 1979 and it is a quarter day when rents are due; some landlords used to hold goose feasts for their tenants. Goose Fairs were a feature of rural areas, the largest being the Nottingham Goose Fair, held on 3 October. Malton Sheep Sale is held at Michaelmas.

In some parts of Yorkshire, ripe rose hips were picked and turned into a drink on Hipping Day while Hiring Fairs were sometimes held. These were mainly held at Martinmas (see 11 November) and were fairs at which hopeful youngsters would assemble in the hope of being hired either as a farm worker or a servant girl.

Miscellaneous Days in September

Clipping Sunday — This has nothing to do with sheep farming and wool clipping, the name coming from *clyppan* meaning 'to embrace'. It involves children encircling their parish church, holding hands and dancing three times around the building after which it is blessed. Church Clipping was held on the Sunday nearest 19 September, although in some areas it was performed on the feast day of the patron saint of a particular church. The custom was recently revived at Guiseley and Tankersley near Barnsley. It seems to have descended from a festival of youth in Roman times and has survived at Painswick in Gloucestershire and Wirksworth in Derbyshire.

Grandparents' Day — Following the success of Mothering Sunday, Mother's Day and Father's Day, the charity organisation, Age

67

Concern in York, decided to hold a Grandparents' Day. The first was in 1990 and it was decided to hold the event on the fourth Saturday in September thereafter. It is designed to encourage young people to appreciate the older members of our society, and to raise funds for Age Concern.

Rush Bearing Day — The first Sunday in September is set aside for Rush Bearing ceremonies at Haworth and Sowerby Bridge (see July and 9 August). At Sowerby, a spectacular rush cart is towed by sixty men in white shirts, black trousers and Panama hats. It passes through hill-top villages in Calderdale, leaving rushes at each church, and there is a service at St. Peter's Church, Sowerby Bridge.

Byland Sunday — On the second Sunday of September, an open air ecumencial service is held in the ruins of Byland Abbey near Coxwold.

OCTOBER

"October always has twenty-one fine days."

Because wine flows in October, the Anglo-Saxons called it Wynamonath, although another name was Winterfylleth, when winter begins. It was once eighth in the calendar, Octo meaning eight and introduced by Romulus in BC 753. It moved to tenth place with the introduction of January and February.

Yorkshire folk examine the weather to foretell the state of the winter; for example, a warm October heralds a cold February, but if October and November are cold, then the following January and February will be mild. Farmers would advise their colleagues:

"In October dung your field
And your land its wealth will yield."

Another belief, prevalent around the Moors, Wolds and Dales, is that if leaves hang on the branches in October and wither without falling, they foretell a frosty winter with much snow. It is said that for every mist in October, there will be a snowfall in the winter, the density of the fog determining whether the respective snowfalls will be heavy or light. In rural areas, it is believed that if foxes bark a lot in October, they are calling a heavy fall of snow.

Days in October

2 October — St. Leger's Day

This saint has no links with the famous St. Leger horse race run at Doncaster during the second week of September. The St. Leger, England's oldest classic horse race, is named after Colonel, later Lieutenant General, Anthony St. Leger who in 1774 suggested a sweepstake of 25 guineas each for three year old horses. The St. Leger, run without a name in its early days, attracted thousands from every part of Britain to Doncaster town moor race course. The race was named after its founder in 1778.

10 October — St. Paulinus' Day; Ganging Day; Queue Day

In AD 601, St. Paulinus of York was sent by the Pope to help St. Augustine with his work in England. A highly successful preacher, Paulinus converted many notable people, including King Edwin of Northumbria and the Druid High Priest Coifi (see my *Folk Tales from York and the Wolds* as by Peter N. Walker, published by Hale). He made Yorkshire history when he baptised more than 10,000 converts in the River Swale near Boroughbridge. He is honoured in York.

In some rural areas, parishioners would tour their parish boundaries on this day to mark them in the memory of the young people, although the more usual date for this was Rogation Sunday (see May).

To mark the arrival of England's first queue, this is Queue Day. The first queue occurred today in 1881 at the Savoy Theatre in London. Queues have survived since that time and can be joined in various parts of Yorkshire.

12 October — St. Wilfred's Day

Wilfred has many links with Yorkshire and is especially associated with Ripon (see August). He spent time in Lyons and Rome and was a spokesman at the Synod of Whitby in AD 664; his defence of the church's links with Rome helped establish the date of Easter (see March) and he was the first Englishman to carry a lawsuit to Rome.

Courageous and intelligent, he became Bishop of Ripon and of York. In 675, he persuaded the Pope to allow Hexham a right of sanctuary and was buried at Ripon. A westerly wind today heralds fine weather.

14 October — National Jogging Day

This was instituted in the United States of America in 1978, but there is no official record to show how many Yorkshire people adopted the habit.

18 October — St. Luke's Day; Dog Whipping Day

Throughout Yorkshire and further afield, it is believed a period of unusually warm weather begins on or near St. Luke's Day. This is St. Luke's Little Summer and may last a few days. Horn fairs are held, the horns being from the ox; the ox is the symbol of St. Luke.

Dogs were also whipped because, centuries ago, one of them misbehaved in York Minster by eating a consecrated communion host. Dogs accompanied their owners to Mass and each church had an official dog-whipper to ensure the good behaviour of canine churchgoers. Dogs found in the streets of York and Hull on this day were also whipped; this might be the origin of the name of York's shortest street — Whip-Ma-Whop-Ma-Gate.

20 October — Yarm Fair

The renowned three-day Yarm Fair sold horses on Day 1, cattle on Day 2 and cheeses on Day 3. It continues as a fun fair, usually beginning on the first Wednesday after 18 October. Yarm left Yorkshire in 1974 to join Cleveland County.

21 October — Feast of St. John of Bridlington; Trafalgar Day

St. John was born at Thwing in the East Riding and died at Bridlington in 1379, being canonised by Pope Benedict XIII in 1401. Following his education at Oxford, he returned home and became a monk, later becoming Prior of Bridlington, earlier known as Burlington. During his life, John was visited by kings, bishops, priests, knights and pilgrims and once saved some fishermen in a storm. Upon his death, the priory became a pilgrim's shrine but was destroyed at the Reformation.

Today is Trafalgar Day when the achievements of Lord Nelson are honoured. Wreaths are laid at his column in Trafalgar Square, London. Of Yorkshire interest is that Viscount Horatio Nelson's mother was from Yorkshire. Catherine Suckling, the grand niece of Sir Robert Walpole, the first Earl of Orford, was the daughter of a farmer at Burnsall in Wharfedale. She married the Rev. Edmund Nelson, rector of a parish in Lincolnshire and they produced a son called Horatio who became England's most famous admiral.

25 October — St. Crispin's Day; St. John of Beverley's Day

There used to be a saying that every Monday was St. Crispin's Holiday. This name was used by people who had Monday off work because they worked Saturdays. St. Crispin's Holiday should not be confused with St. Crispin's Day; St. Crispin is the patron saint of shoemakers. For details of St. John of Beverley, see 7 May.

31 October — Hallowe'en; the Eve of All Hallows; the Eve of All Saints; Samain; Winter's Eve; Allantide; Ash Ridding Night; Hodening Horse Day; Nutcrack Night; Snail Tracing Night; Witch Lating Night; Trick and Treat Night

This continues to be a mystical evening. In the Christian church, it is the Eve of All Hallows, hallows being an old word for saints, while in the pagan world it is Samain, the last night of the year and the night of their greatest fire festival. It is dedicated to the dead. The pagans believed the ghosts of their ancestors returned home and elaborate preparations were made to welcome them.

Huge bonfires were lit to strengthen the sun and ashes were scattered upon agricultural land to promote fertility. In the north of England, and in parts of Yorkshire, these bonfires were lit even into the last century. Now, the fires have been transferred to 5 November which we call Bonfire Night, and we have nominated York-born Guy Fawkes as the object of our fire lighting.

In fairly recent times, Hallowe'en games were played, one of which was dipping for apples. Apples floated in a barrel of water and had to be seized by the teeth while the player's hands were tied behind the back! Nuts were used by rural girls to divine the name of their future husband; they were marked with the names of pairs of lovers and placed near the fire. If the nuts spat away due to the heat, they were examined to see whose names they bore. It was considered any such couple were incompatible. Nuts which remained near the flames were thought to indicate the peace and tranquillity of marriage. (See 28 and 29 September). Snails were also used to divine the names of loved ones — a snail was placed in a closed dish overnight. The marks it made were supposed to be the initials of one's future spouse.

At Whitby, love-sick youngsters climbed the tower of St. Mary's Church to shout the names of their intended across the sea. Their destiny was assured if, at the sound of the name, bells sounded from beneath the waves. The bells had been stolen from Whitby Abbey when it was dissolved by Henry VIII, and lost at sea. (See my *Folk Tales from the North York Moors* as by Peter N. Walker — Hale). The bells are still there!

In the Pennines, Witch Lating Night was celebrated by a person going up to the moors between 11 pm and midnight while bearing a lighted candle. If the flame burned steadily, it signified the person carrying it would remain free from witchcraft for twelve months. If the flame went out, great evil would attend that person! Ash riddling was also conducted — ashes were riddled and left in the hearth overnight. If a footprint appeared, the person who fit it would die within a year!

In Cornwall, the night is known as Allantide when apples are given to every member of a family to ensure good luck, but a new practice has crept into Britain. It is Trick and Treat from America. (See 1 and 4 November). Children tour the houses and ask "Trick or treat?" If some gift of money or sweets is not given, then mischief is perpetrated — this includes smearing grease or paint on doors, the removal of gates or garden ornaments or other pranks. Children wear witches' masks or carry turnip lanterns during their rounds, a relic of pagan times.

Miscellaneous days in October

Conker Days — These are held at differing times, but usually in October and the purpose is to determine the local conker champion or even the World Conker Champion. Conkers are the ripe fruit of the horse chestnut and when suspended on a length of string or a shoelace, they are used to batter the conkers of an opponent. The champion is the one which beats all others. Secret recipes toughen one's conkers, but packing them with concrete or Yorkshire grit is forbidden.

NOVEMBER

"A cawd November, a warm Kessimus."

November was called Windymonath by the Anglo-Saxons because winds often occurred; fishermen also drew their boats ashore for the winter. One rather unpleasant name is Blodmonath, blood month, because livestock were slaughtered for winter meat. In the Roman calendar, this was the ninth month, hence the prefix of *novem*, but the addition of January and February made November No. 11.

Throughout Yorkshire, it is said that flowers blooming in November herald a harsh winter and many November sayings relate to the weather. "Ice in November brings mud in December" is one while another is "A cold November brings a warm Christmas". To these we can add,

"If there be ice in November that'll bear a duck,
There'll be nowt after but sludge and muck."

The November verse of Thomas Hood (1799-1845) is often quoted:

"No warmth, no cheerfulness, no healthful ease,
No comfortable feel in any member,
No shade, no shine, no butterflies, no bees,
No fruits, no flowers, no leaves, no birds — November!"

Days in November

1 November — All Saints Day; All Hallows; Hallowmas Day; Hallow Rood Day; Caking Night

Today the church honours saints for whom no particular day has been established.

Many churches are dedicated to All Saints and by long tradition, this was when all deceased persons, whether saints or not, were remembered in the Mass of the Day. Church bells tolled to reinforce the mourning and in some areas, this atmosphere of gloom continued tomorrow, All Souls. In some places, mischief was

74

practised, but that custom has been transferred to either Hallowe'en (31 October) or Mischief Night (4 November). In the West Riding, this was Caking Neet or Night because soul-cakes were distributed for All Souls' Day.

An ancient piece of weather lore says that if the beech mast is dry on All Saints, we shall have a hard winter. If the mast is wet, a damp winter is expected.

This day has been called All Hollands or All Hollans which is a corruption of All Hallows, and the period around it is called Hollantide. It can be unexpectedly mild and a popular saying goes:

"If ducks do slide at Hollantide, at Christmas they will swim;
If ducks do swim at Hollantide, at Christmas they will slide."

2 November — All Souls Day; Hodening Day

Before the Reformation, prayers were said for the souls in Purgatory; this was a stopping place en route to heaven where sinners paid a penance before acceptance. In many parts of England, particularly the north, soulers went around the villages singing hymns to earn alms or cash which would pay for Masses for their deceased relatives. Prior to this day, Yorkshire ladies would make huge amounts of soul cakes, sometimes called Saumas Loaves (Soul Mass Loaves), to give to the soulers — these were simple scone-like productions with added spices. At Stannington near Sheffield the soulers were called guisers because they disguised themselves with blackened faces.

In some cases a Hodening Horse toured the houses. This was a man covered with a sheet and carrying a horse's skull. Accompanied by a party of youths, he would tour the houses to raise soul money or donations of soul cakes. Any money raised was used for Masses for the Dead. Afterwards, there was a good natured fight to secure the horse's head which was then given a mournful funeral.

These souling traditions have died out in Yorkshire, but I believe a variation continues in Cheshire. Children with blackened faces tour the houses singing mournful songs with a view to earning a few pennies — but the cash is for themselves, not for the souls in purgatory!

4 November — Mischief Night

The northern part of North Yorkshire, along with Cleveland, Durham and Northumberland has long tolerated Mischief Night. It appears not to be celebrated in the southerly parts of Yorkshire except for a small area in the south west of the county. Gangs of youngsters tour the towns and villages playing pranks on householders or upon anyone who happens to encounter them. Garden gates are taken off hinges, butter, lard or treacle smeared on door knobs, letter boxes sealed, windows rattled or door bells rung before the householder emerges; shop windows are whitewashed and similar tricks are played. Over the last decade or so, vandalism has developed and police forces issue stern warnings that no damage or vandalism will be tolerated and that perpetrators will be prosecuted.

The law is not suspended as some believe. In many areas, much of the mischief has been transferred to Hallowe'en in the form of trick and treat. See 31 October and 1 November; also see February for Nickanan Night, Dappy Door Night and Lent Sherd Night.

5 November — Guy Fawkes' Night; Plot Day; Bonfire Night; Tar Brush Night

Guy Fawkes was born in York and in 1605 died a horrible death at the age of 36 for his alleged part in a plot to blow up the Houses of Parliament. In fact, the bonfires of Hallowe'en (31 October) were transferred to this day so we now light them to commemorate the ghastly torture of a young man who was probably innocent of the charges against him. St. Peter's School in York, where Fawkes was educated, does not partake in the celebrations neither does his home village of Scotton near Knaresborough.

Elsewhere, bonfires are lit either in domestic gardens or as part of community gatherings; these are accompanied by colourful displays of fireworks along with food, drink, music and sometimes dancing.

In some moorland villages, yard brooms were stolen and soaked in tar before being set on fire. Youths then raced around carrying these blazing brooms. In other parts of the north, tharf cakes were eaten. These were spicy buns and their purpose is obscure. In the dialect of the North Riding, tharf means shy or diffident, but it is possible the cakes were linked to the Norse god Thor whose feast day was on or about 5 November.

Known in parts of the West Riding as Plot Day, roast potatoes, ginger parkin and parkin pigs (pig-shaped parkin biscuits) are eaten. Home made Plot Toffee is also made. A peculiar verse was sung on the North York Moors in which the effigy of Fawkes was known as Awd Grimey. The verse was:

76

"Awd Grimey sits upon yon hill,
As black as onny awd crow;
He's sitten on his lang grey coat
Wi' t'buttons doon ti t'flooer."

7 November — St. Willibrord's Day

Born in Yorkshire and educated at Ripon, St. Willibrord became Archbishop of Utrecht in Holland and is buried in Germany. Hornsea and Hedon held hiring fairs today.

9 November — Lord Mayor's Day in London

Although this was once the day for electing the Lord Mayor in London, mock mayors were elected in towns and villages of other parts of England. Kilburn near Thirsk elected a mock mayor for Kilburn Feast (see July). Non-Yorkshire mock mayors had to tour the inns to partake of free offerings of ale until they were unable to stand. This conduct matches a feature of London's Lord Mayor's Day when the Mayor's jester was compelled to leap, fully clothed, into a vat of custard.

11 November — Armistice Day; Remembrance Day; Veterans' Day; Martinmas Day; Martlemas; Martlemas Beef Day; the Feast Day of St. Martin of Tours; Pack Rag Day; Poppy Day; Stattis Day

King George V suggested the commemoration of the dead of World War I by ceasing all normal activities for two minutes at the eleventh hour of the eleventh day of the eleventh month. This became the two minutes' silence. The armistice which ended that war was signed at 11 am on 11th November, 1918 and the day was called Armistice Day. Now, the dead of the second World War and other conflicts are commemorated upon the same day which is known as Remembrance Day; services of remembrance are held on the second Sunday of November. In America and Canada, it is Veterans' Day. The Field Poppy, a red flower which grew on the battlefields of Flanders after World War I, is the symbol of Remembrance Day. Real and artificial poppies are worn; one variety is named after Somnus, the god of sleep.

Today is the feast of St. Martin of Tours, otherwise known as Martinmas or Martlemas Day. Martin was bishop of Tours in France for more than 50 years and died in AD 397; in the sixteenth century, French Protestants destroyed his shrine at Tours. In some English rural areas, Martinmas is still celebrated on 23 November, this being brought about by the calendar changes of 1752. It was an important day for country folk, being the day rents were paid, accounts settled and new tenancy agreements made. Hiring fairs were held throughout Yorkshire (see 29 September), when labourers and domestic servants trekked into town to seek work, and the occasion was one of feasting, drinking and general amusement. When servants sought new work, they packed their bags and left their place of residence — thus the day became known as Pack Rag Day.

The name Stattis Day is a corruption of Statutes Day, (see 25 November) when conditions for hiring farm workers were laid down by statute. In some areas, the day was known as Martlemas Beef Day — enough beef for the coming year was placed in household chimneys to cure. A short period of warm weather sometimes begins around this time and is known as St. Martin's Little Summer. There is a saying that if the geese stand on ice at Martinmas, they will walk in mud at Christmas; another says that if Martinmas is fair, dry and cold, the cold in winter will not last.

12 November — the Morrow of St. Martin's Day

Potential sheriffs are nominated; the final selection is on 3 February.

13 November — Bull Running Day

Over the Yorkshire borders in Lincolnshire until 1839, bulls were turned loose in the streets of Stamford and chased by dogs and men with sticks.

17 November — St. Hilda's Day; St. Hugh of Lincoln; Queen's Holiday

Hilda, one of Yorkshire's best known saints, was abbess of Whitby Abbey. Born in AD 614, she was a member of the Northumbrian royal family (see 20 August) and became Abbess of Streonshalh (Whitby) in AD 657. She supervised the famous Synod of Whitby in AD 664 which had been summoned to determine whether the English branch of the church adopted the traditions of Rome or those of the Celts. The Roman tradition was accepted and this determined the method by which the date of Easter continues to be calculated. (See Easter Sunday — March).

Many Yorkshire churches, Protestant as well as Catholic, have St. Hilda as their patron but her relics disappeared at the Reformation.

At Egton near Whitby, a specially composed hymn is sung on St. Hilda's Day. Comprising ten verses, the first is:

"Sing the glory of our patron,
Blest St. Hilda, Virgin free;
Child of wild Northumbria's monarch,
Spouse of Christ she chose to be."

The author is unknown, but the tune is "Daily, daily."

Today is also the feast of another local saint, St. Hugh of Lincoln; a French Carthusian monk, he was sent to Lincoln by Pope Urban III in 1174, and upon becoming bishop in 1181, began to rebuild the Cathedral.

Today is also The Queen's Holiday — Elizabeth I, that is!

22 November — St. Cecilia's Day

St. Cecilia is patron saint of musicians and on this day, concerts are held throughout Yorkshire, this custom being recently revived in her honour. The Worshipful Company of Musicians goes in procession to a service at St. Paul's Cathedral, London. No-one knows why she was chosen as patron saint of musicians, although legend says she invented the organ, composed hymns and possessed a good singing voice.

23 November — Clementing Day; St. Clement's Day

Blacksmiths and children would go Clementing on this day, but not necessarily together. For the blacksmiths, this entailed parading through the village with an effigy of Old Clem and the children would visit houses to ask for money or gifts after reciting verses or singing songs. Clem suppers and clem cakes were popular. The patron saint of tanners, St. Clement is said to have succeeded St. Peter as Pope in AD 68, although some authorities specify the date as AD 91, with Linus and Cletus reigning between Peter and Clement.

24 November — Cutting Off Day

The day before St. Catherine's Day when lacemakers cut off the pieces they had been working and sold them. The next day was a holiday.

25 November — Catterning Day; St. Catherine's Day

St. Catherine, a beautiful and intelligent woman, was martyred by being lashed to a spiked wheel which turned in different directions and ripped her to pieces. The Catherine wheel, a type of firework, is named after this wheel. On St. Catherine's Day, or Catterning Day as it has become known, Cattern Cakes were eaten. An old verse says:

> "Rise, Maids, Rise,
> Bake your Cattern pies,
> Bake enough and bake no waste,
> And let the bellman have a taste."

As St. Catherine is the patron saint of lacemakers, they had a holiday on this day. Until the 1920s, a team of farmworker dancers, the Rotherham Statutes, performed upon this day. (See Statis Day, 11 November)

30 November — St. Andrew's Day; Andermas; Squirrel Hunting Day

St. Andrew is the patron saint of Scotland because, it is said, some of his relics were taken to that country by a monk and buried in the town which is now called St. Andrews. It was a squirrel hunting day in Kent and the famous Wall Game is played at Eton. The day was sometimes called Andermas, a Mass being celebrated in honour of St. Andrew.

Miscellaneous Days in November

Remembrance Sunday — see 11 November

Stir-up Sunday — This is moveable and falls on the Sunday before Advent. The name comes from the collect of the day which begins, "Stir up, we beseech thee, O Lord, the wills of thy faithful people." Country women believe it is the day to stir Christmas puddings and it was considered a fortuitous day for making them. At the Anglican church of St. James at Lealholm in the Esk Valley, the ladies raise money by stirring Christmas pudding mixture and selling it for church funds.

Advent Sunday — is the fourth Sunday before Christmas and the beginning of the church year. It falls around St. Andrew's Day.

End of Flat Racing Day — The week containing 22 November marks the end of flat racing in this country.

Rive Kite Sunday — This is the Sunday following Martinmas Day and the Hiring Fairs. Farm workers and servant girls were given a celebratory meal before leaving for their new employment. Rive Kite means a split stomach, an indication of the size of the meal.

Parkin Sunday — In the West Riding, on the Sunday within the octave of All Saints (1 November), peppercake made from treacle and ginger was eaten. This was called a parkin.

Driffield Hiring Fair — On the Thursday nearest 23 November, celebrated by some as Martinmas Day, Driffield held its hiring fair.

DECEMBER

"A December cold with snow is good for rye."

The name comes from *decem* meaning tenth month but the Anglo-Saxons called it haligmonath, holy month. It was also known as wintermonath, the month of winter.

Weatherwise Yorkshire people believe that "Thunder in December presages fine weather" and if it rains before Mass on the first Sunday in December, it will rain for a week.

Days in December

6 December — Old Christmas Day; St. Nicholas' Day

It is from St. Nicholas that the nickname Santa Claus is derived. St. Nicholas was a kindly bishop at Myra and gave presents in secret to the needy children. Today was Christmas Day in the Julian calendar and in some countries, presents are given.

11 December — the start of the Halcyon Days

The Halcyon Days continue for fourteen days and are supposed to bring mild, calm and pleasant weather as well as great happiness and prosperity. Some authorities state the Halcyon Days begin on 14 December. Halcyon is the Greek for kingfisher; legend said the bird nested on the sea during this calm weather and so the period became known as the Halcyon Days.

13 December — St. Lucy's Day

There is an old verse which goes:

"Lucy light, Lucy light,
Shortest day and longest night."

This is a puzzle because, even allowing for differences caused by the old calendar, St. Lucy's feast day is not the shortest day. Her name does mean light, however, and she is the patron saint of glaziers. In Switzerland, Lucy is depicted as the wife of Father Christmas.

20 December — St. Thomas' Eve

Ghosts roam free from the Eve of St. Thomas until Christmas Eve. Lovesick Yorkshire girls would try to establish the identity of their future husband. Before going to bed, a girl had to peel a large red onion and stick nine pins into it. One had to go in the centre with the others around it. As the pins were pressed home, she had to sing this rhyme:

> "Good St. Thomas, do me right,
> Send my true love to me tonight,
> In his clothes and his array
> Which he wearest every day,
> That I may see him in the face,
> And in my arms may him embrace."

Having done this, she had to go to bed and place the onion, complete with pins under her pillow. She then hoped she would dream about her future husband.

The carol singing season begins today.

21 December — St. Thomas' Day; Gooding Day; Shortest Day; Candle Auction Day

Boys from the North York Moors would go A-Thomassing today. This meant visiting outlying houses to ask for St. Thomas gifts, usually a piece of pepper cake or Christmas ginger bread with cheese. In some areas, poor women would tour the mills to beg portions of wheat which were ground free of charge so they could make Christmas cakes. In return, they gave gifts of holly. This was known as A-Gooding.

There used to be a Yorkshire belief that any girl marrying today was destined to quickly become a widow. Another custom was that St. Thomas' onions, or shallotts, were planted and some felt it was a good day to plant broad beans. In some rural areas, candles were auctioned in preparation for winter; candle auctions also occur when lots are sold as a candle burns away.

At Richmond, the Mayor's Audit Money is distributed to the poor around St. Thomas' Day. Pensioners collect it from the mayor's house, and have tea and biscuits.

Today is the winter solstice — longest night and shortest day.

24 December — Christmas Eve; Ashen Faggot Day; Dumb Cake Day

There is an old belief that cattle, horses and sheep sink to their knees at midnight in honour of the birth of Christ and that hived bees hum the psalms.

Frumetty, also known as frumenty, is a porridge-like dish customarily made on Christmas Eve from pearled wheat (wheat in the husk) or barley which has been *creeaved* the previous night. This entails soaking it in water until it swells.

In some parts of West Yorkshire, the wheat husks were crushed, or kibbled, before being soaked. On Christmas Eve, the wheat is cooked slowly with equal parts of milk and water; three hours or so seems to have been the normal cooking time and it was eaten on Christmas Eve, before going to Midnight Mass.

When hot, frummety was flavoured with things like sultanas, raisins, spices, cinnamon or even rum, sherry or brandy. Sometimes it was followed by a piece of cheese with a cross on top.

Another important Christmas Eve custom was to bring in the Yule log. This was the remains of last year's Yule log; it was used to ignite a new log of long-lasting wood which was supposed to continue smouldering until Christmas Day or even longer. A small part was kept until the following year and used to light the new Yule log. If the Yule log stopped burning, it indicated bad fortune for the household. Some massive Yule logs in the great country houses were kept burning throughout the Twelve Days of Christmas.

In some parts of the country, an ashen faggot was used; this comprised a large bundle of ash sticks bound together and lit with the remains of last year's ashen faggot.

At All Saints Church, Dewsbury, the Devil's Knell is tolled. It begins at midnight and consists of one stroke for every year since the birth of Christ. By tradition, it is to keep the Devil at bay. Some 2000 tolls takes rather a long time!

Love sick girls would make a cake out of flour, water, eggs and salt at midnight on Christmas Eve, and then eat it. After walking backwards upstairs, it was thought she would see a vision of her future husband. This was called a dumb cake.

Robin Hood died this day in 1247 and his tomb is at Kirklees near Brighouse — so the legend says.

25 December—Christmas Day; Apple Wassailing Day; Bean Planting Day

Youths, known as shouters or waits, would tour villages on Christmas morning and were responsible for rousing those who wanted a sleep-in on this holiday. They would stand at the door and shout:

> "I wish you a merry Christmas and a Happy New Year,
> A purse full of money and a cellar full of beer.
> Two fat pigs, and a newly-calved cow,
> Good Master and Mistress, how do you do?
> Please will you give me a Christmas box?"

There were local variations of that verse and I remember shouters chanting similar lines in the 1930s and 1940s in Yorkshire's Eskdale. A similar verse was used in the East Riding. Older women, known as Vessel Singers, would tour the houses carrying a doll in a small box. The doll was dressed as the Virgin Mary and was surrounded by things like red berries, sweets or cakes; sometimes, there were three dolls representing the Holy Family. These boxes were sometimes called Milly Boxes, a derivation of My Lady Boxes. Touring within the last fifty years, the Vessel Singers, a corruption of Wassail Singer, would sometimes repeat these lines as they sought cash or gifts:

> "God bless t'Maister of this house,
> And his mistress too,
> And all the little bonny bairns,
> That roond thy table go.
> And all thy kith and kindred,
> That dwell beeath far and near,
> And Ah wish you all a Merry Christmas
> And a Happy New Year."

At Boroughbridge towards the end of the century, waits toured the town singing and playing musical instruments throughout the Christmas period. The practice might have originated in watchmen doing their rounds and attempting to be cheerful. A similar custom occurred at Stokesley, while at Pickering the waits were accompanied by a shouter whose duty was to rouse sleepy householders. One of the verses they sang was:

"Good morning, Mister Capstick,
Good morning, Mrs. Capstick,
And all the little Capsticks —
It's five o'clock and it's a frosty old morning."

Apple trees are sometimes wassailed on Christmas Day and some gardeners believed that broad beans should be planted between now and 6 January, ie during the twelve days of Christmas, although some planted them on 21 December. It was also a quarter day when rents were due.

One widespread belief is that children born on Christmas Day will be extremely gifted.

26 December — St. Stephen's Day; Boxing Day; Wren Hunting Day; Bleeding Day

This is the day King Wensleslas looked out and saw the snow lying crisp and even as a poor man gathered winter fuel in the midst of a cruel frost. Wrens were hunted and killed, supposedly because their loud singing aroused the jailer just as St. Stephen was about to escape.

The name of Boxing Day is a puzzle. One theory is that presents were packaged and given to tradespeople, but a more likely explanation is that collection boxes in churches were opened on Christmas Day and the contents, ie the box money, was given to the poor on Boxing Day.

At Sheffield, two groups of sword dancers perform while wearing military tunics and there is also a sword dance at Flamborough. Tug-of-war contests are held across the River Nidd at Knaresborough and bathers in fancy dress enter the sea at Whitby. There are many sporting events ranging from fox hunting to football, including a cricket match with strange rules at Thornton Watlass near Bedale.

It was also known as Bleeding Day because cattle were bled in the belief that it was beneficial to their health, and in North Yorkshire, it was thought that cattle knelt in honour of St. Stephen's martyrdom.

28 December — Childermass Day; Holy Innocents' Day

Mass was said for children slaughtered by King Herod during his hunt for the infant Jesus.

The day has been celebrated since the fifth century, and church bells are muffled. It was considered the unluckiest day of the year, and children born today were thought unlikely to survive. No new enterprise should be started — no weddings, no new jobs, no new clothes — nothing in fact. It was even thought unlucky to clean the house or to cut one's fingernails.

31 December — New Year's Eve; Hogmanay

Most of the celebrations of this evening occur in the north of the country, the further north one goes, the more intense the activity! The Scots love Hogmanay and there are events like Burning the Clavie (a barrel of tar) in Morayshire and a Fireball Swingings Day in Kincardineshire. Northumberland enjoys a Tar Burning Day in Allendale while many other regions settled for more apple wassailing, or apple howling, when cider was thrown over apple trees and lots of noise made with guns, drums and blasts from a cow's horn.

In Yorkshire, New Year's Eve is celebrated with varying amounts of gusto; in bygone times, rural folk would eat the remains of the frumetty, while nowadays, the pubs and clubs host parties to "see in the New Year". It is customary to kiss as many handsome people as possible at the stroke of midnight. Even today, First Footing or Lucky Birding is practised after midnight (see 1 January).

Miscellaneous Days in December

Scripture Cake Day; Bible Sunday — This is the second Sunday of Advent when Scripture Cake was eaten. Popular with Dales folk, this cake was also enjoyed on outdoor picnics and other occasions.

This was a very rich fruit cake whose ingredients are to be found in the scriptures — eg 4.5 cups of 1 Kings IV v22 (flour);
1 cup of Judges V v25 (butter);
2 cups of Jeremiah VI v20 (sugar);
2 cups of Nahum III v12 (figs);
2 cups of 1 Samuel XXX v12 (raisins);
2 cups of Numbers XVII v8 (almonds);
1.5 cups Judges IV v19 (milk);
6 of Jeremiah XVII v11 (six eggs);
2 tspn of 1 Samuel XIV v25 (2 tspns honey);
2 tspns of Amos IV v5 (2 tspns baking powder);
a pinch of Leviticus II x13 (salt) and to taste,
2 Chronicles IX v9 (spices).

UNCLASSIFIABLE DAYS

Among the days said to have been celebrated in Yorkshire, especially in pubs, are the following. No dates are given due to the moveable nature of these important occasions nor is it known whether they are weekly, monthy, annual, spasmodic or the figment of someone's imagination.

Bucket Carrying Day, Pea Pushing Day, Wellie Chucking Day, Billiard Table Jumping Day, Custard Pie Heaving Day, Egg Waltzing Day, Ferret Legging Day, Potato Casting Day, Cheese Rolling Day, Dwyle Flonking Day, Snubbit Cleaning Day, Rhubarb Thrashing Day, Passing the Splod Day, Conger Cuddling Day, Sun Wading Day, Nettle Wrestling Day, Flither Picking Day, Bottle Kicking Day, Uphod Saturday and Hare Pie Sunday.